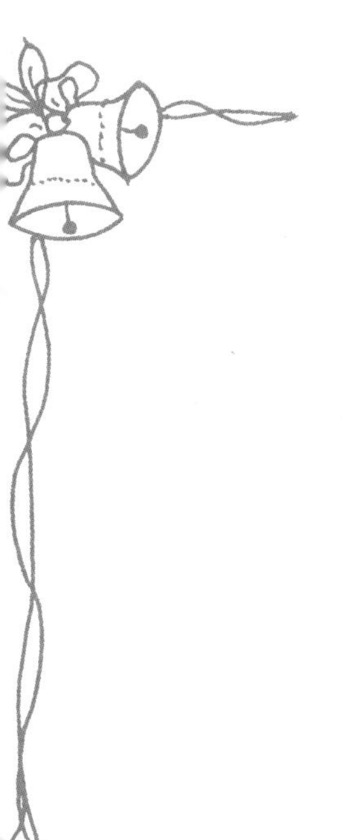

MILNER CRAFT SERIES

Folk Art Wedding

JOYCE SPENCER

SALLY MILNER PUBLISHING

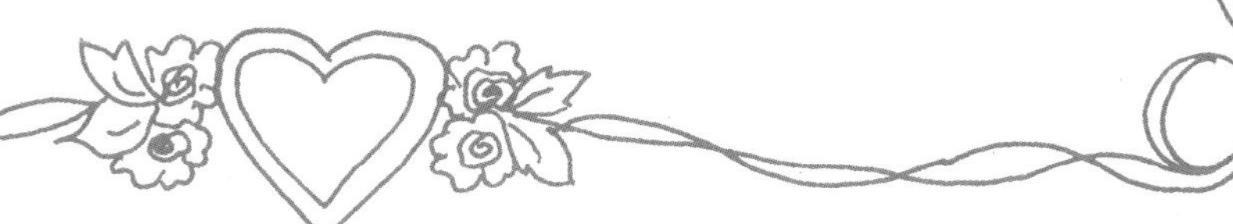

By the same author
The Art of Teaching Craft by Joyce Spencer and
Deborah Kneen, Sally Milner Publishing 1993
Folk Art Cards, Sally Milner Publishing, 1993
Folk Art Ceramics, Sally Milner Publishing, 1994
Milner Craft Series

First published in 1997 by
Sally Milner Publishing Pty Ltd
at The Pines
RMB 54 Burra Road
Burra Creek NSW 2620 Australia

© Copyright, Joyce Spencer, 1997

Design by Anna Warren
Styling by Deborah Kneen
Photography by Glenn A Keep
Printed in Hong Kong

National Library of Australia
Cataloguing-in-Publication data:

Spencer, Joyce
    Folk art wedding
    ISBN 1 86351 202 0.
    1. Wedding decorations. 2. Folk art. I. Title. (Series: Milner craft series).
745.5941

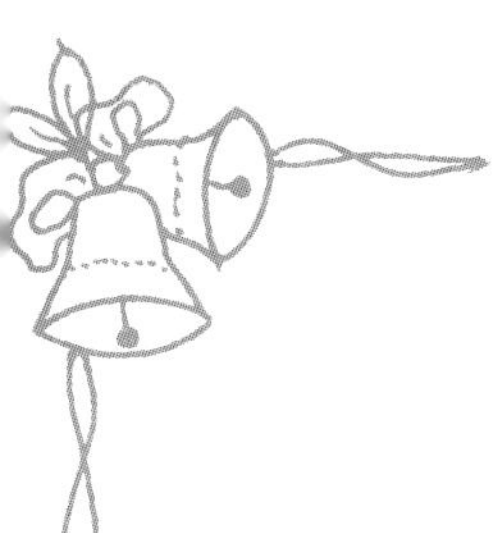

CONTENTS

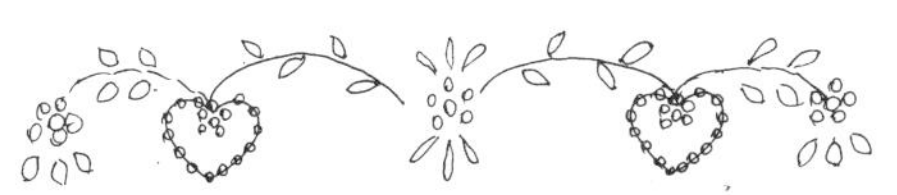

Acknowledgements 4
Introduction 5
Equipment and Materials 7
Paints and Mediums 9
Brushes 11

PREPARATION OF PAINTING SURFACES 14
Sanding, Sealing and Basecoating 16
Stroke Painting and Other Brush Techniques 18
Creating Painted Backgrounds 27
Stencilling and Templates 33
Tracing the Design 35
Lettering 36
Using Moulds 37
Finishing Techniques — Antiquing and Varnishing 39

PROJECTS

BRIDE'S PAINTING PLANNER 42

BOXES AND MORE BOXES 47
Bride's Best Undie Box 47
Bride's Bath Box 49
Groom's Gear Box 53

SMALL RING AND GIFT BOXES 56
Pink Heart Ring or Gift Box 56
Hearts and Doves Ring Box 58
Antiqued Gold Leaf Cherub Gift Box 61

HALF POTS AND POTS 63
White Bisque Half Pots for Pews 63

Green Half Pots for Pews:
Sponged Pot and Wisteria Pot 64
Peach and Gold Cherub Pot 65
Blue Lapis Lazuli Pot 66

CHERUBS AND ANGELS 68
Painted Chocolate Bowls 68
Rainbow Rice or Rose Petal Bowl 70
Simply Striped Candle 73
Gold Leaf Candleholder 74

WEDDING INVITATIONS AND PLACE-CARDS 77

BOOTS, SHOES AND HORSESHOES 79
Lucky Boot 79
Pink Champagne Slipper 81
Shoes to Match Bridal Train 82
Good Luck Horseshoes 84

FOR THE CAKE 86
Cake Stand 86
Granny's Old China Knife 88
Blue and Gold Strawberry Cake Tray 90

FRAMES AND MORE FRAMES 93
Old Silver Frame 93
Gold, Pearl and Pewter Frame 95
Granite Photo Frame (or is it?) 96

COATHANGERS 99

PAINTED TRAIN 101

RESORT CASE 108

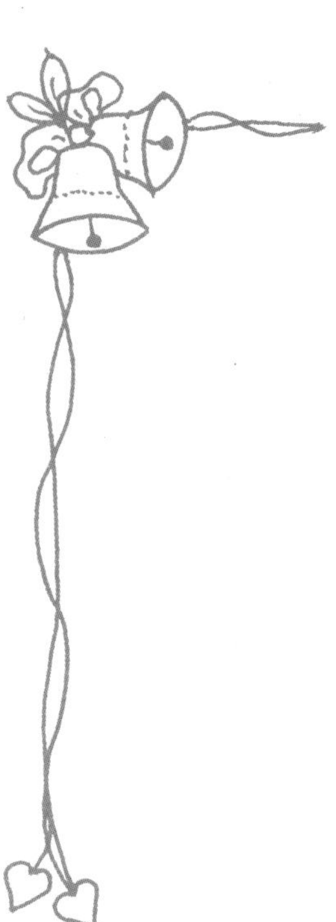

ACKNOWLEDGEMENTS

Once again, I am indebted to Sally Milner and her staff for publishing this book, and to my friend Deborah Kneen for her wonderful styling which allowed photographer Glenn Keep to shoot at a tremendous and record-setting pace. This would not have been possible without the help of Phyll Hill, Deb's Mum, who kept us nourished and under control. Thanks also to Yvonne Hunter of The Cake Company, Hurstville, Sydney who decorated the cake featured on the cover.

A very special mention to my husband Geoff, who always gives me lots of support.

However, it was the marriage of our daughter, Llewellyn, which prompted the production of this book. In preparing for her wedding to Gary, we all wanted something different and special for this memorable occasion. Of course, not every project in this book was made for the wedding, but there were enough painted items to give to each female guest. Gary became a great chocolate maker, the glue gun became my best friend, and shopping became great fun seeking out those numerous types of cherubs, angels and decorative bits and pieces.

Special events are definitely enhanced by T.L.P.— Tender Loving Painting — especially weddings.

JOYCE SPENCER 1997

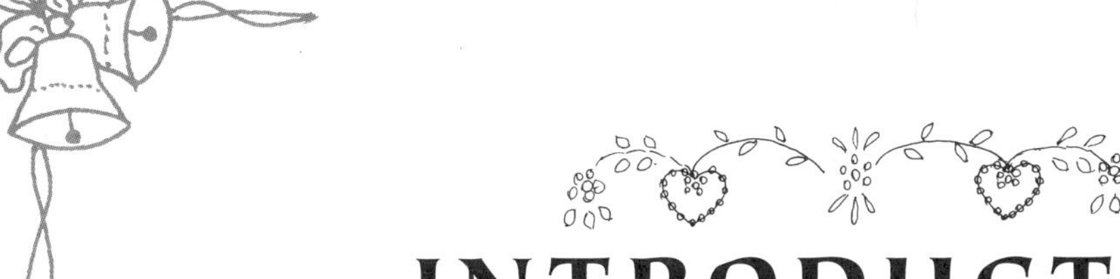

INTRODUCTION

This book is about painting various items for your wedding. It tells you how to paint pieces that will make the occasion more decorative, colourful and individual. It is about creating treasures, establishing traditions and setting your own style.

Every bride wants her wedding day to be memorable, every minute enjoyed and treasured by the bride and groom, their families and friends. Yet the day passes so quickly, and it is often in the preparations and anticipation that much of the pleasure lies. Creating these painted items will enrich the time leading up to the wedding, giving the bride-to-be, her family and friends the opportunity to make their own unique contribution to the special day.

My daughter said to me, 'Mum, I don't want a painted wedding!' 'Of course not, dear', I replied. 'But perhaps just one or two little things?' (Like the wedding invitations, the cake stand, the chocolate bowls, the rose petal bowl, the pew decorations and so on.) A wedding is a time for indulgence.

But even if you are not as extravagant as me and you manage to paint only one or two items from this book, you will have made a wonderful effort and gained a great deal of satisfaction from the process. I know that brides are busy people. They are often working and have little time to prepare for the big event. But why not ask for help from your family, friends and relatives? People love to help and its is fun to paint with others.

The instructions and information are written for the those who have never painted before. Should you have a close relative or friend who paints, you are indeed lucky. The painting can then be shared, learnt and taught along the way. There may even be time for you to take folk art classes. But if you have

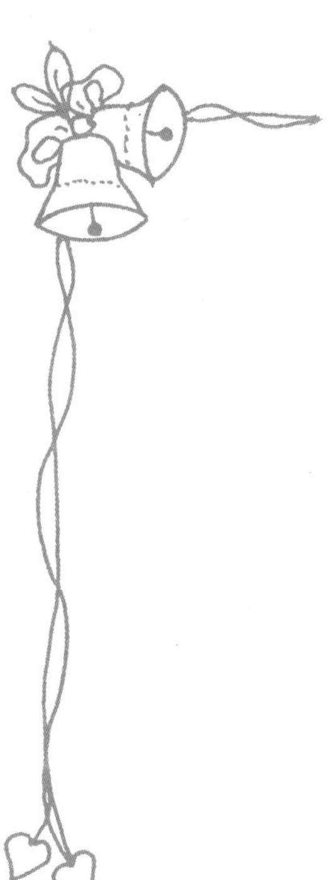

never held a brush, take heart. By following the step-by-step instructions, and choosing a simple piece to start with, you will soon be painting with confidence and developing new skills.

The Bride's Painting Planner has been designed with the beginner in mind. It is a painting sampler and it includes all the techniques, which are explained in great detail. On completing this sampler, you will find most of the projects in this book will be easy.

Good luck, and best wishes. Have a very happy painted wedding.

JOYCE SPENCER, 1996

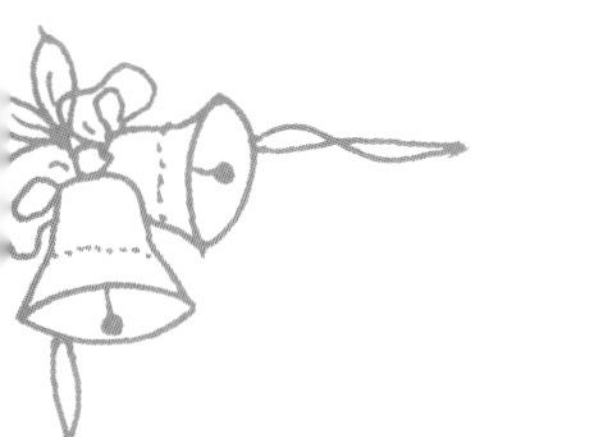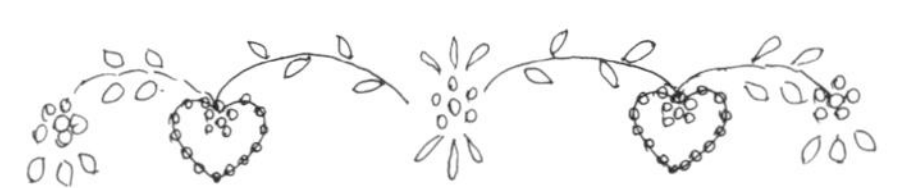

EQUIPMENT AND MATERIALS

G ENERAL NEEDS INCLUDE:

Cloth, to protect work surface

Disposable gloves

Wet and dry sandpaper

Pencil

Notebook

Ruler

Scissors

Cardboard

Craft glue or glue gun

Scrap paper

Greaseproof paper

Fine-point pen

Magic tape

Plastic lids or old saucers, to be used as palettes

Wooden sticks, for mixing paint

Glass jar

Basin

Paper towels

Cotton buds. for removing 'mistakes'

Old toothbrush, for spattering

Sponges, as listed

Plastic wrap

Nail brush

Cheap brushes

Feathers

Hand soap, for cleaning brushes

Brush cleaner

Soft absorbent rags, tack cloths

Detergent

Cotton balls

Apart from paint and brushes (refer to Paints and Mediums on page 9 and Brushes on page 11), you will need these art supplies:

Sealer, such as Jo Sonja's All Purpose Sealer

Carbon pencil

Saral paper

Graphite paper

Stylus

Palette knife

Stencils

Paper

Gold Leaf

Silver Leaf

Mediums

Varnish

Suppliers

Suppliers include art shops, craft shops, folk art shops, ceramic studios, garden shops, hardware stores, bridal supplies, florists, supermarkets, discount shops, cake decorating shops and party shops.

I bought the cake stand from Mr Don O'Neil, 27 Carabella Road, Caringbah, NSW 2229. You will find old cases and shoes at St Vincent de Paul and Salvation Army shops. Angels and cherubs can be found floating around all the above-mentioned outlets.

Setting up to paint

Finding a suitable place to paint is not always easy, but a wedding takes precedence and anything is possible. I use the kitchen counter and keep my painting things in a cupboard. You can keep a box containing your equipment under the bed, if that is the only space available. Protect all painting surfaces with plastic (especially if you are painting on the dining-room table!).

You will also need to find storage space for the finished items. Store with plastic, not paper, between the pieces, unless they are completely dry.

It is a good idea to make a shopping list of everything you need for the piece you are going to paint. A lot of the items can be found around the home. Saucers or plastic lids make good palettes. Old toothbrushes, household sponges and plastic wrap can be used for different effects. Only buy the paints you need for a particular piece. You can add other colours as you go along.

Set up the painting space with your chosen piece and all the equipment needed to complete the article. Keep old jars filled with water close by. Keep a notebook and pen for reminders and for jotting down any ideas that pop into your head. Keep brushes upright in a jar. Have some paper towels and a few cotton buds handy in case of mistakes. Use only small amounts of paint at a time. Cover any leftover paint with plastic wrap to keep fresh.

You are ready to start painting.

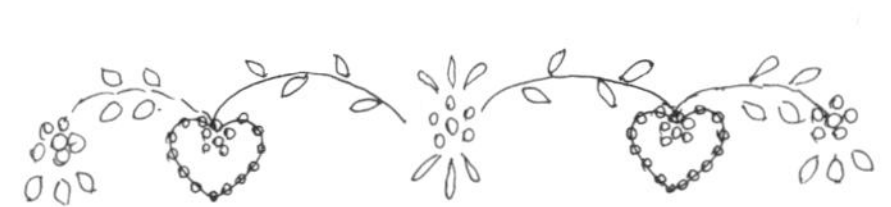

PAINTS AND MEDIUMS

Folk Art Paints

Most of the paints used for the designs in this book are water-based acrylics specially formulated for folk painting. The colour range is enormous and colour charts are available to assist you when searching for a particular colour. Folk art paints come in plastic bottles and tubes.

Base coat Paints

Base coat paints are specially formulated to flow. The colour range is good, and the large bottles make painting several items with the same colour economical.

Fabric Paints

There is an acrylic paint made specifically for painting on fabric, but folk art paints can be used once a textile medium has been added. In fact, some folk art paints do not need this medium and can be used straight from the bottle. It is vital to read all instructions, and to do a sample piece first. Mix any paints that need a textile medium and keep in a small container if a quantity is to be used. Otherwise, you can add the medium as you paint.

Most fabric paints require heat setting, using an iron or a hair dryer. Refer to *The Painted Train* on page 101 for instructions.

Dimensional Paints

Dimensional paints are mostly used for fabric painting, but in the last few years I have been using them on paper and for folk painting. These dimen-

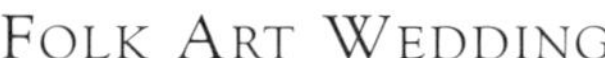
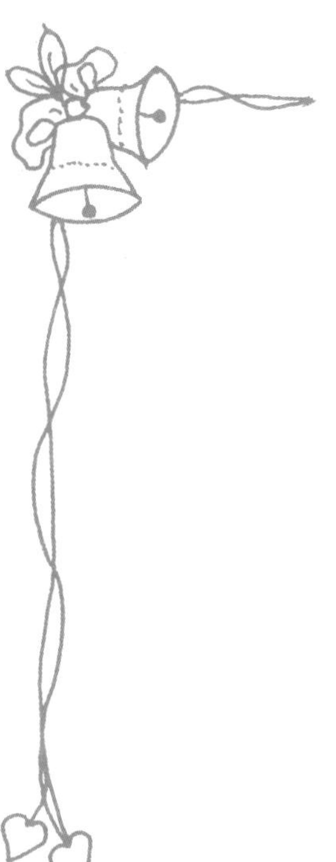

sional paints do not necessarily need to be applied with a brush, as they come in small bottles with plastic applicators attached. The paints are available in many colours and textures, smooth iridescents, adhesive-based glitters, pearls and metallics.

Texture Paste

This is another dimensional paint that resembles snow or clouds. It is applied to the angels and bow on the lid of the Bride's Bath Box. When dry, it can be painted over with colours, or a glitter or crystal paint. Please read all labels. Sometimes a long drying time is needed.

Glitter Paints

Glitter paints are mixed in an adhesive base, so it is wise to clean all brushes thoroughly with soap and water. Take care not to allow the glitter surface to come in contact with another surface, as they will stick together. Glitter paints have a long drying time.

Metallic Paints

These paints are available in an exciting colour range — pearls and coppers, golds, silvers and many other colours. They can be used as a basecoat on their own or like a wash for a transparent effect. Alternatively, paint a matching colour first, then apply the metallic colour for an opaque and lustrous finish.

Mediums

A medium is a specially formulated substance added to paint which slows down the drying time of the paint, acts as a glue or makes the paint flow better. I usually use Jo Sonja's mediums, and all are available from art, craft and folk art shops. For more interesting effects, particularly using Kleister medium, I would refer you to my *Folk Art Cards* book.

All mediums used are listed for each project.

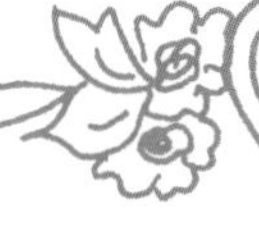
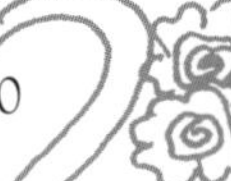
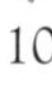

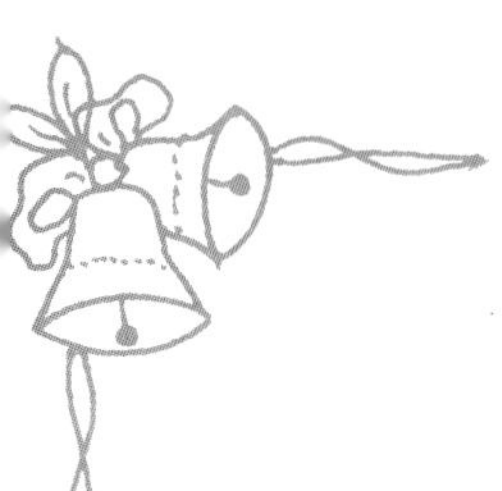

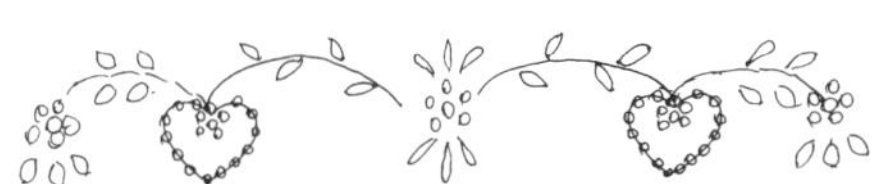

BRUSHES

The following brushes are used in this book. Painting instructions and diagrams to help with the strokes and functions of each brush are in the section called Stroke Painting and Other Brush Techniques (see page 18).

Most folk art brushes have a short wooden handle, a metal ferrule and the size, the manufacture and type of bristle stamped on the handle.

The ferrule is shaped differently from brush to brush. The shader, for instance, has a flat ferrule, and the liner brush has a very small round ferrule. The bristles for our purposes are synthetic.

Brush Care

If you clean your brushes after every use, they should last a long time. Swish the brush in a small glass of water, run it over some hand soap, then swish again to remove the soap and paint. If the water colours, there is still paint in the brush. (Clean sponge in the same way using a basin of water.) Never leave paint in a brush, even for half an hour, and never leave a brush sitting bristle end down in a jar of water. Always stand the brushes with the bristles up in a jar.

Basecoat Brushes

Various types of brushes can be used for basecoating:

- **sponge brushes.** These do not last long, but they cover well, and come in all sizes. 1" is quite suitable.

- **long-handled cheap Chinese brushes.** Suitable sizes are ½" – 1".

- **No. 1 Francheville 250 Taklon.** This is my

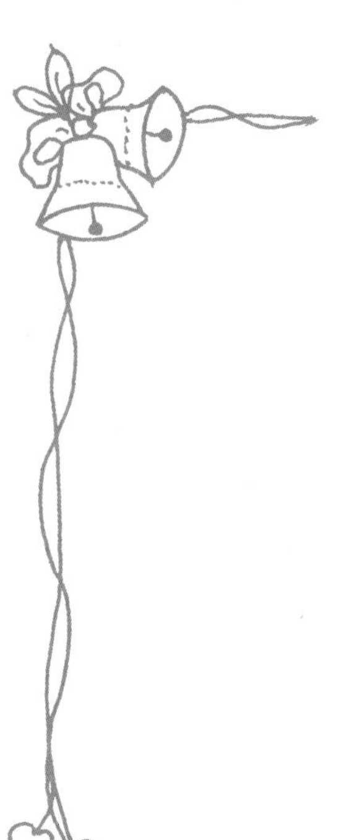

favourite basecoating brush.

- **flat brush** ¼"
- **comb or rake brush** ½" (Only used for the Resort Case)
- **round brushes.** Nos 1, 3, 5 and 8 are good for painting shapes.
- **stencil brushes** (refer to Stencilling on page 33).
- **sponges.** Ceramic or sea sponges or torn car sponges are excellent basecoaters.

Round Brushes

The round brushes vary in size from very small 00 to quite large. Use the smaller brushes for very detailed work, and the larger brushes for washes or very large strokes. For the projects in this book, the following brushes are used: Nos 3, 5 and 8. All of these make lovely strokes, and they can also be used for stencilling, basecoating shapes and washes.

Remember: the smaller shape or stroke, the smaller the brush, the larger the shape or stroke, the larger the brush.

Flat, or Shader Brushes

A flat brush has a flattened metal ferrule, holding the synthetic bristles. The flat brush used for the projects in this book is a ¼". It is used to paint small buds and roses with a method called flat brush blending.

Dagger Brushes

These little treasures of brushes are favourites of mine. The metal ferrule is flat but the bristles are cut at an angle. (There is also an angle brush but the dagger brush has a more acute angle.) Two sizes are used — the ⅛" and ¼". Dagger brushes require frequent rinsing and cleaning, because the paint is kept down near the ferrule and tends to clog. The dagger brush is used frequently for painting leaves

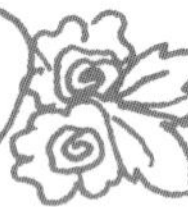

in the designs in this book. The Blue and Gold Strawberry Cake Tray has groups of the larger leaves made with the ¼" brush.

Fine Liner Brushes

I use a 00 Round Liner brush for detailed work and outlining. The hairs are longer, which means that they hold more paint. Pressure can be applied and strokes are possible. This brush makes bows and ribbons and is good for writing and lettering.

For very detailed painting, there are small round brushes with shorter bristles.

A script liner is a similar brush, except that the hairs are longer and, for a new painter, harder to manage.

Scungy Brushes

These are old, worn-down, hardened with paint and have matted bristles. They are useful for many techniques, such as the faux lapis lazuli on the Blue Lapis Lazuli Pots. To make your own scungy brush purchase a cheap Chinese pig bristle brush, size 1 or 2. Cut the long bristles short with scissors and pound the brush up and down in the paint before using. Remove excess paint on a paper towel and dab lightly where needed. The result is a fine, hairy-like effect.

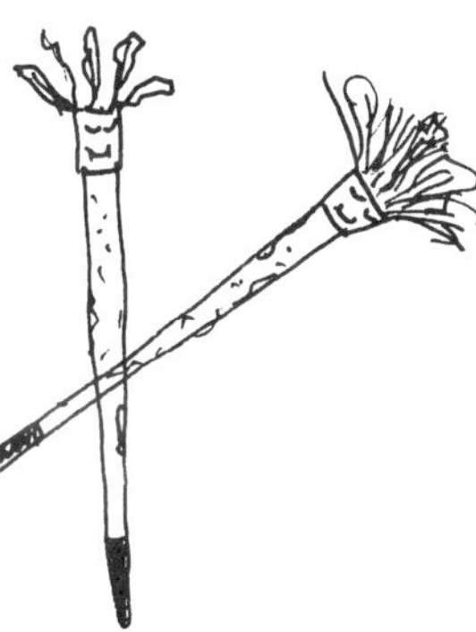

SCUNGY BRUSHES

PREPARATION OF PAINTING SURFACES

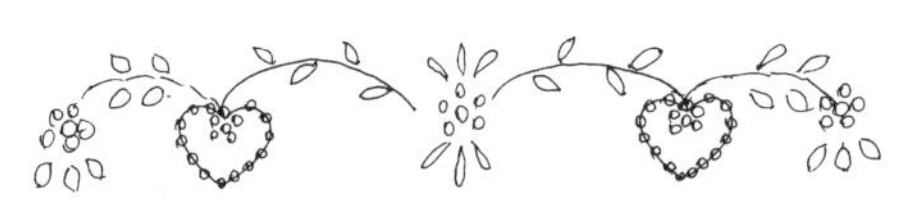

When we pick up a painted object, we automatically run our hands over the surface. Any roughness and poor preparation will not be covered up by varnish.

Papier-Mâché

Papier-mâché items are used a lot in this book. The cost is reasonable, and the surface requires no preparation and is easy to paint. The Bride's Bath Box is the exception here. A sealer, and two or more coats of varnish are applied to make the box waterproof.

Paper

The paper used for the invitation needs no preparation.

Terracotta and Ceramic Bisque

Terracotta is porous, which means that it absorbs water. So, if you are applying a basecoat, you will have to seal all terracotta items first. Seal them inside and out. Jo Sonja's water-based sealer is ideal for this purpose.

Ceramic surfaces also need to be sealed. Mix the sealer with the basecoat to make it easier to apply.

Timber and Craftwood

Timber and craftwood surfaces require sanding and sealing. Check the item at the time of purchase, and reject it if it is too rough and will require too much preparation.

To sand, fold a small piece of 'wet and dry' sandpaper and sand gently in one direction, not around and around. If the edges are routed, fold paper again and again and work backwards and forwards, getting into the grooves.

Wipe off any wood dust with a tack cloth, which is available at a paint or craft shop

Apply the sealer with a brush or sponge. I use Jo Sonja's water-based sealer, which is suitable for many surfaces. Please read the label. Sealer can be mixed into folk art paints if basecoating a small item. Folk Art basecoats usually have the sealer formulated into the paint. Sand very lightly after sealing.

Metal

The only metal used in this book is on the Bride's Painting Planner and the Resort Case. Scrub off any rust with very fine steel wool. To remove any residues, paint with a 50:50 mixture of water and vinegar. Dry well before applying an all-purpose sealer. Now the metal is ready for basecoating.

Leather

Painting on leather is fun, especially if the surface is textured. If old, the leather needs to be scrubbed with water and detergent, then dried well in the sun. Glue down any little tears. For large items like cases use water-based varnish and folk paint. For smaller items like shoes you can use leather sealers and paints from shoe repairers..

Fabric

Do not dry-clean the fabric before painting. Wash the fabric and iron out all creases. Please refer to the Painted Train on page 101 for full instructions on painting fabric and use of Textile Medium.

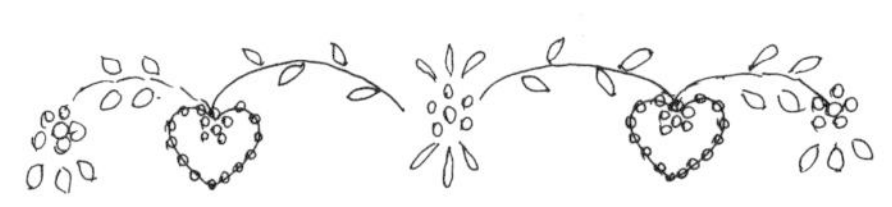

SANDING, SEALING AND BASECOATING

Sanding

Sanding is most important. I mostly use a sheet of fine wet and dry type glass paper from the hardware shop. I divide the paper into small pieces and fold it over, which allows me to get into any grooves. It is best to sand in one direction, then sand in the opposite direction rather than go round and round. Please refer to Timber and Craftwood surfaces on page 14.

Sealing and Sealants

A folk art sealer is a special formula either added to the paint or painted on the surface before basecoating to either make the paint adhere better or to give it protection from rust and dampness. We can also apply a coat of sealer between painting techniques such as sponging, spattering and faux finishes. It is necessary to read labels thoroughly, as some folk art paints already contain a sealer.

The sealer needs to be applied with suitable brushes and painted evenly and lightly sanded. If there are any ridges in the dried sealer, they will show through the basecoat paint.

The same brushes used for sealing can be used for basecoating.

Basecoating

Basecoating is a very important painting step. It refers to painting the foundation on which you will place your design, or to filling in the various elements of the design — the petals or leaves — with a single colour. For example, the instructions might say to 'basecoat the petals pink'. This means to fill in the petals with pink folk art paint, painting over, say, a white basecoat.

Unless I have stated otherwise, I have used the larger containers of FolkArt basecoat. These are more economical when painting several items with the same colour. Jo Sonja's acrylic paints and other brands in small plastic tubes or bottles are also suitable, but you may need to mix a little sealer with them. Read the labels and ask for any information at the shop if in doubt.

Set up a painting space. Put down an old towel or sheets of paper where you are going to paint. Have a basin of water to one side if using a sponge and sponge brush, as water may be needed to thin the paint a little. You will also need paper towels to mop up any mistakes and wipe the brushes, and a clean tack cloth. Shake and mix the paint well before pouring onto a small plastic tray or small container. Only practice will be the guide as to how much paint to use. Set up a drying area to one side and have the hair dryer ready.

1. Apply the first basecoat, using a sponge brush or a wide, flat nylon bristle brush. Flow the paint onto the surface, making sure all your strokes go in the same direction. Try to avoid creating ridges, which are usually caused by too much paint being applied.

2. Allow to dry. Paint one side first, allow to dry, then paint the other side. Do not place items wet with paint onto newspaper or towels. I have a painting board, with fine nails sticking up, on which I place freshly painted items. You could rest the item on drawing pins stuck into a piece of cardboard.

3. When dry, sand lightly, wipe off any dust with the tack cloth and apply a second coat. This time, stroke in the opposite direction.

4. Run your hand over the dried paint to test for smoothness. Another light sand and wipe may be needed.

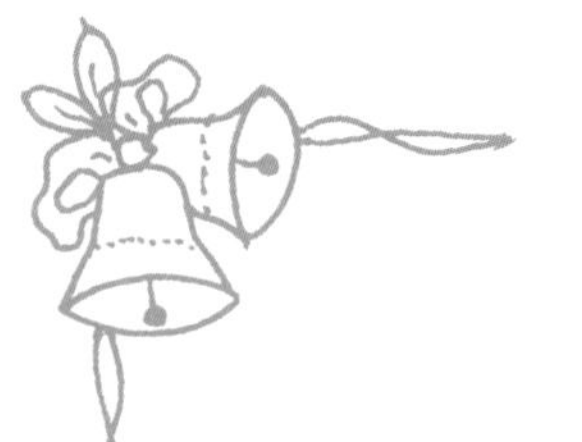

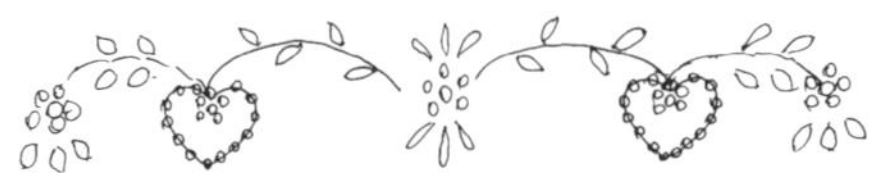

STROKE PAINTING AND OTHER BRUSH TECHNIQUES

Folk painting in the traditional way, requires the mastery of strokes relating to a specific style from a country in Europe. Each country has a name for its style; for example, a style of stroke painting from Bavaria is called Bauernmalerei, while a distinctive style from Holland is called Hindelopen. You could spend a lifetime studying every known style and technique.

These origins and styles form the bases of our contemporary style of decorative painting, although different paints, surfaces, mediums and brushes are used. I do recommend that, if you have taken to folk painting, you study, take classes, and join the many hundreds of happy painters who belong to groups and associations.

I find stroke work very relaxing, but you have to have everything in place. Use the correct brush — small brushes for small strokes. Mix the paint to correct consistency. Set your work in the right direction for the stroke. Have pleasant designs to paint. Find a comfortable place to paint, with warmth or cooling, good lighting, a cup of coffee and music if desired.

STROKE PAINTING

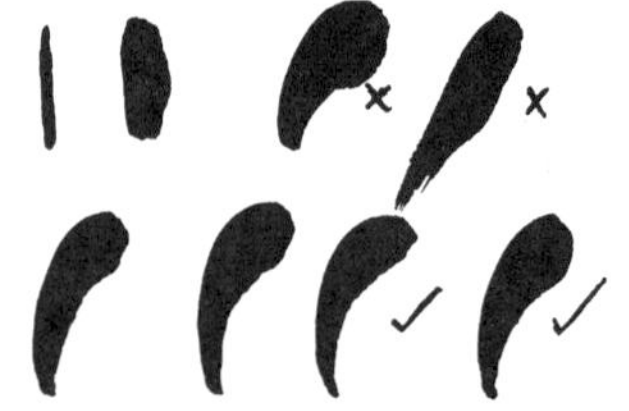

comma stroke

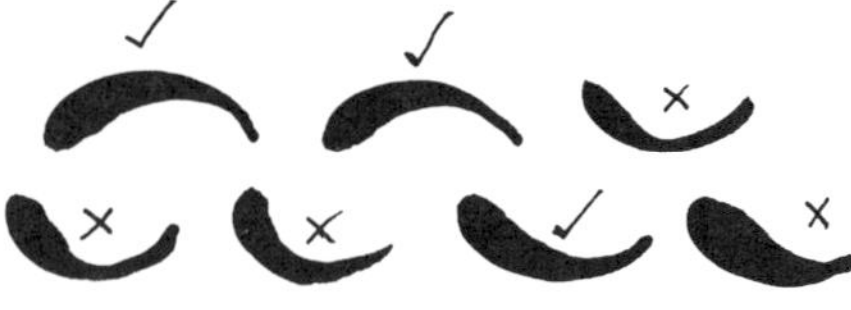

eyebrow stroke

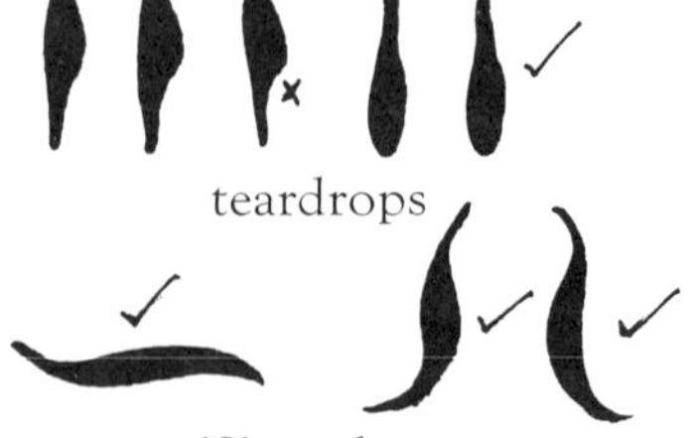

teardrops

'S' strokes

Comma Strokes (Round Brush)

A stroke synonymous with the Bavarian style is the comma stroke. This stroke is the basis of folk painting. To practise this stroke, you will need a No.3 round brush, a palette, water, paper towels and practice paper.

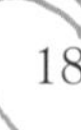

1. Squeeze a small amount of paint onto the palette.

2. Dip a round brush into the water and use this to mix some paint. (When practising, this is acceptable but when painting, the paint should be mixed with a palette knife. Paint mixing does shorten the life of the brush.)

3. Holding the brush like a pencil, take up some paint into the brush — this is called loading the brush. Support your hand if necessary, as you are going to roll your hand to the left, to the right and pull down and up to make this stroke.

4. Place the tip of the brush gently down on the paper, and lift. You will have made a blob. Place the tip of the brush down again and apply pressure, noticing how the bristles widen. Reload with paint after every stroke.

5. Place the tip down again, applying pressure at the same time, then pull straight down to make a stroke. Reload the brush, place the tip down while applying pressure, pull down a little way, then release the pressure. This time there should be a wide brush mark at the top narrowing to a thin line. We call these strokes 'teardrops'. And whether they go to the right or left, up or down, or look like eyebrows, they are all comma strokes.

It is the combination of applying and releasing pressure, in the direction you want the stroke to go, that makes stroke painting work.

Double-Loaded Strokes (Round Brush)

Double loading means to carry two colours on the brush at the same time. Use the following colour combinations: green/white, white/green, blue/gold, gold/blue, and so on. If you use a lighter colour for the second colour, you will create a highlight. You will also need a No.3 or 5 round brush, a palette, water, paper towels and practice paper.

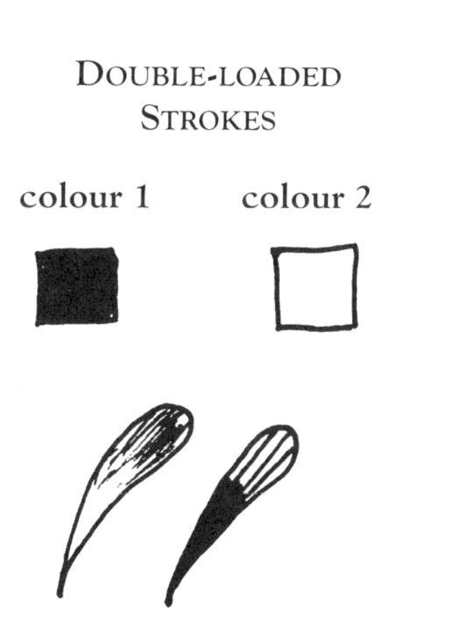

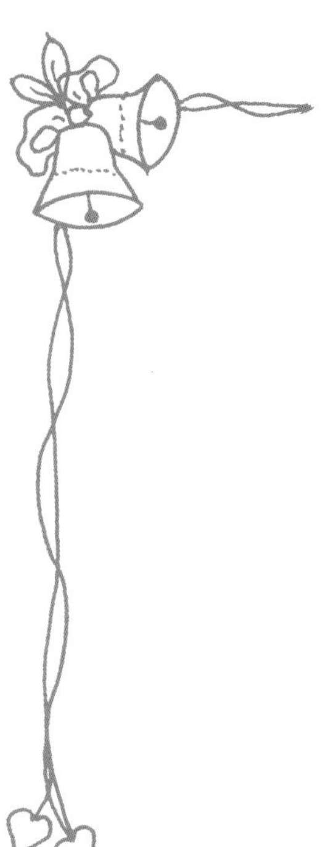

1. Load the base colour onto the brush, then dip the tip into the contrasting colour, picking up a little paint.
2. Paint the stroke. There should be a tip of contrasting colour at the top and a striped stroke.

Reload the brush every time to get the right amount of paint on the brush for the stroke. If you don't do this, eventually the paint mixes on the brush to a paler colour.

Round Brush Blending

Round brush blending is a method of applying light and shadow to a shape. My method of blending is illustrated on the Blue and Gold Strawberry Cake Tray. Please refer to the Colour Plate, and assume that you are going to paint a blue strawberry. The basecoat colour is Ultramarine Blue, the shading colour is Storm Blue and the highlight is White. You will also need a No.3, 5 or 8 round brush, and a palette. A retarder 'medium' can be used to aid blending. Add retarder to paint or paint a shape, then blend.

1. Using a large round brush, basecoat the strawberry. Allow to dry.
2. Apply Storm Blue on the right side of the berry. Wipe the brush.
3. Apply White on the left side of the berry.
4. Wipe off excess paint on a paper towel and blend up and down on the light side and over to the darker side, getting rid of the line down the middle. The result should be an interesting mix of different values of blue and the effect of light and shadow on the strawberry.

  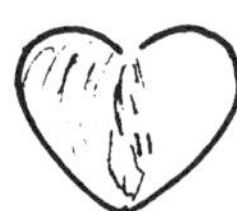 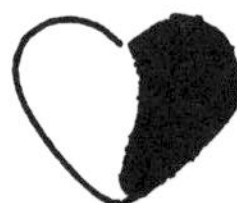 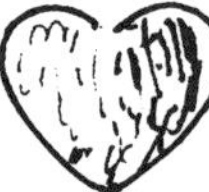 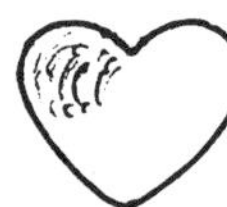

trace   basecoat   light   shade   blend   highlight

ROUND BRUSH BLENDING

 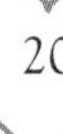 

5. To further 'highlight' the light area and make it appear as though the light is striking that point, lightly dry brush a little White over the top left corner (see Dry Brushing on page 26).

The process can be repeated until you are happy with the result.

When blending, the piece needs to be turned or set up for painting in the right direction. When I blend the centres of the heart flowers, for instance, I paint the shading down from the centre, towards me, then turn the plate up and blend the highlight down towards the centre.

Flat Brush Blending — Buds and Roses

To paint buds and roses, you will need two contrasting colours, say Plum Pink and Titanium White, a palette, water, paper towels, blending paper such as greaseproof paper, and practice paper.

1. Place the two colours on the palette like putting toothpaste on a brush.

2. Dip your brush into water and dab off lightly on a paper towel. You need to retain a little water in the brush.

3. Holding your palette close to you, pick up a little pink paint on the corner of the brush. Flip the brush over and pick up a little white on the other corner.

4. Blend lightly on the greaseproof paper, working the brush backwards and forwards on a strip 1 cm (⅜") long. Keep the white on top and the pink on the bottom and only ever blend up towards the white. Otherwise the paint will be just a mix of pink and white, ending up a pale pink. Pick up more paint and blend again in the same place. You should now have sufficient paint to paint several buds. If you need more water on the brush, pick up only a little bit, then blend. If the colour mixes, you will have to wash the paint out from the brush and start again. Because you

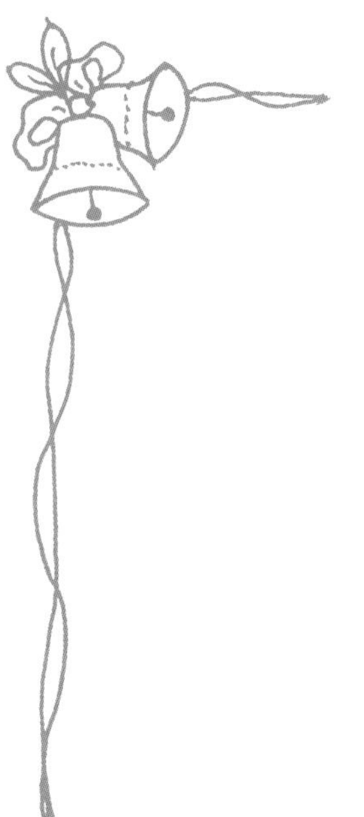

are using a small brush, you will need to blend frequently. When you use a large brush, you will be able to take up more water and paint into the brush, and the blend will last longer.

5. The bud is painted first. Hold the blended brush with the white on top. Put the brush down on the chisel, or fine edge. Pull the stroke up in a fine line and over to the right and stop on the chisel edge. You should have created half an oval. With the white on top, put the brush down on the chisel edge, and go down and up in a curve, applying a little pressure as you go to flatten out the bristles and apply the colour. You should have created a bud. The bottom of the top stroke makes the shading inside the bud. Dab some white dots in the centre with a liner brush or stylus and, when dry, paint three quick small strokes in green or another colour for leaves and a stem to complete the buds. They look better painted in clusters.

6. Now paint a rose. Turn the work to one side and pull a small short stroke across the bud, from left to right, with white to the outside. Then stroke from right to left and flick in a small stroke at the bottom. The petals need to look as though they tuck in under the bud and look attached.

I have used more buds than roses in the book, because for a beginner painter, roses require endless practice. They are the most difficult flower to paint in a blended manner, but if you relax, and understand the process of blending the paint on the brush, and turning your brush to the correct angle, all rose painting is possible.

Dagger Leaves (Dagger Brush)

Practise these leaves on scrap paper first. Once you have mastered this stroke, there will be no stopping you — there will be leaves everywhere. Practise

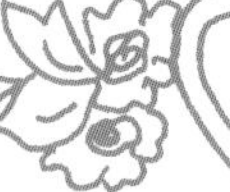
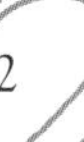

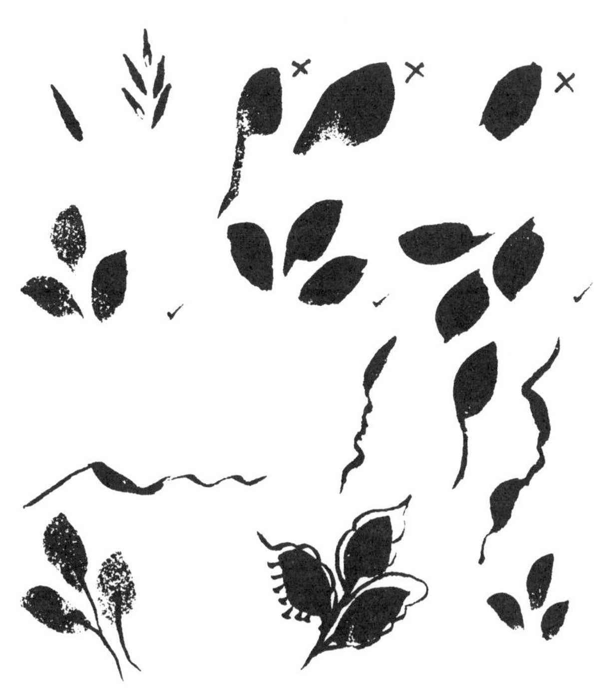

painting them in groups of three, to resemble rose leaves. Single ones look lovely along the LAFS trails (see page 25).

To practise these leaves, you will need a ⅛" dagger brush, a palette, water, paper towels and practice paper.

1. Set out some paint on the palette, mix with a little water and take up some paint into the brush. Holding the brush like a pencil, place it lightly down on the paper. Make a narrow stroke. Arrange these strokes in a pattern and you have some fern leaves.

2. Reload the brush, place it lightly on the paper, and pull it to the left and stop. You should have a leaf with no tail. Repeat, pulling the brush to the right, and stop. You should have another leaf with no tail. It is best to paint veins and stems in a different colour with the liner brush.

3. For more interesting leaves, place three colours, say gold, blue and white, close together on your palette. Pick up a little from each colour along with a dab of water and paint some leaves. The colour combinations are lovely.

4. You could also dilute the paint into a washy consistency with water and paint lots of leaves to create a very interesting misty background, then add more paint for the foreground leaves.

Liner Work — Fine Lines, Borders and Dots (Liner Brush)

Fine white outlining is featured in the design on the Rainbow Rice or Rose Petal Bowl.

When doing linework, you can use flow medium instead of water to dilute the paint. Flow medium aids the flow of paint without diluting any of the colour, which water does. Mix the paint with a few drops — a little goes a long way.

You will also need a 00 round liner, a palette, paper towels and practice paper.

1. Dilute the paint with flow medium or water. You are after a thin mix.

2. Roll the tip of the brush around in the paint so that it takes up more paint. You need to have enough paint in the brush to make quite a long stroke, such as is needed for LAFS trails (see page 25), or a small bow. More than one colour can be put onto the brush, but remember that the paint needs to be thinner. Remove any excess paint on a paper towel.

3. Hold the brush like a pencil and practise writing your name, and doing some bows, and some tick leaves. Apply more pressure to the bristles to make thicker lines, and less pressure for finer lines. A useful stroke for bows and ribbons and the tips of leaves is made with a fine line, no pressure and then pressure, ending with no pressure and a fine line.

Dots

Dots of varying sizes are made by picking up paint on the tip of a stylus, a pin head, a toothpick or

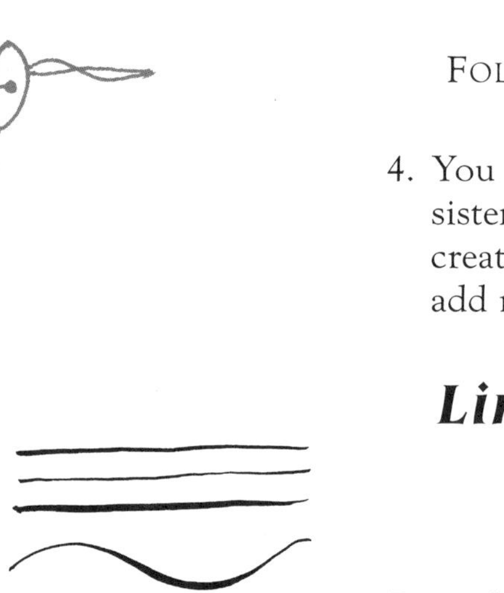

trails

squiggles, tick leaves

outlining

dots

bows

flow medium needs

LINER WORK

DOTS

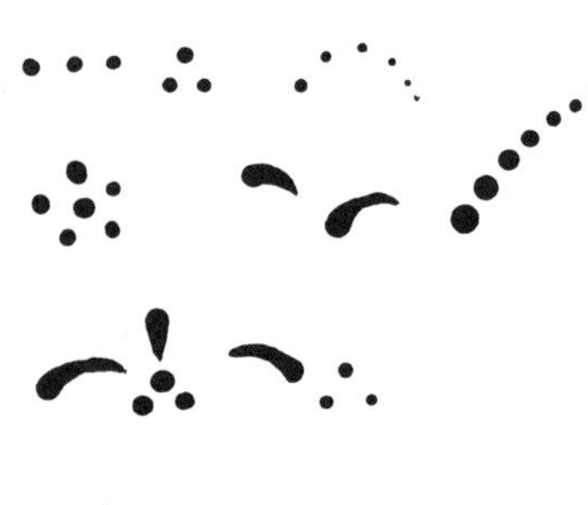

satay stick, and gently placed on the design. The dots make small flowers, borders, and tiny comma strokes.

Filler Flowers

These are made with a small round brush loaded with two colours, such as blue and white. Push the tip of the brush down lightly and make five quick strokes in a circle. Push another colour such as yellow into the centre and you have little forget-me-nots or filler flowers to take up any little gaps in your design.

LAFS Trails

Light Airy Fairy Style (LAFS)

I devised this style of painting to teach beginner students to paint in a free manner with no tracing. Beginners often find traditional strokes difficult to master initially, so this method introduces them to techniques that give instant results. The Bride's Painting Planner is an excellent learning piece that incorporates the LAFS. Full instructions are given (see page 42).

1. Paint three trails of lines under and over one another, using the liner brush.

2. Paint some ribbon trails using the dagger brush. Pick up paint, make a fine line, apply pressure and draw over to one side, then release pressure, continue the fine line and apply pressure and go over to the other side, release pressure and end with a very fine tail.

3. Paint small leaves with a small dagger brush.

4. Paint along these trails with different flowers, buds, roses, ribbons and dots using the round brush, a stylus and different stroke techniques. Relax and enjoy the flowing style.

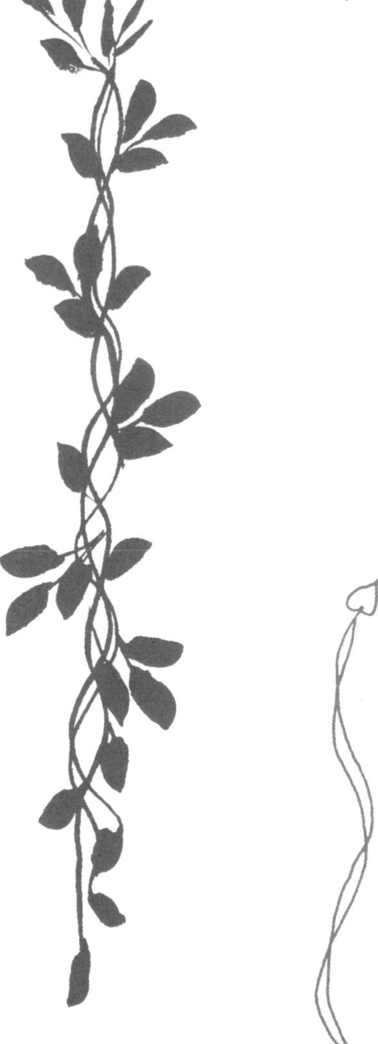

Washes
(Round Brush)

Washes are colours diluted with water until they become transparent. Washes can be used to put in a little shadow or outline a shape — (see the bows and angels on the Bride's Bath Box), or to colour over an entire area (see the Rainbow Rice or Rose Petal Bowl). Different-coloured washes can also be used on top of each other. For large areas of wash, use a large round brush. For smaller areas, such as on the Wedding Invitation, use a smaller brush.

You will need a brush and two jars of water — one for washing the brush and one for mixing the paint. Only a small amount of paint is needed. I use a white plate as a palette, because the depth of colour shows up better. Wipe off between colour changes with a paper towel. Cotton buds are useful to mop up any mistakes and runs.

Dry Brushing
(Round Brush)

Dry brushing is painting with a dry brush and a little paint. The idea of this technique is to apply wisps of colour with a very light touch of the brush to highlight a particular spot. An example is shown on the Blue and Gold Strawberry Tray.

Using a suitable-size dry brush, pick up a small amount of paint and blend back and forth on a paper towel, then lightly brush the area to be highlighted. Do not wash the brush between colour changes, only when finished.

DRY BRUSHING

dry brush colour

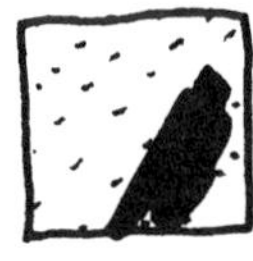

wipe paper towel

too heavy

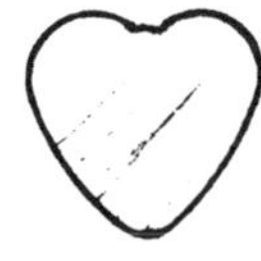

light dry brush

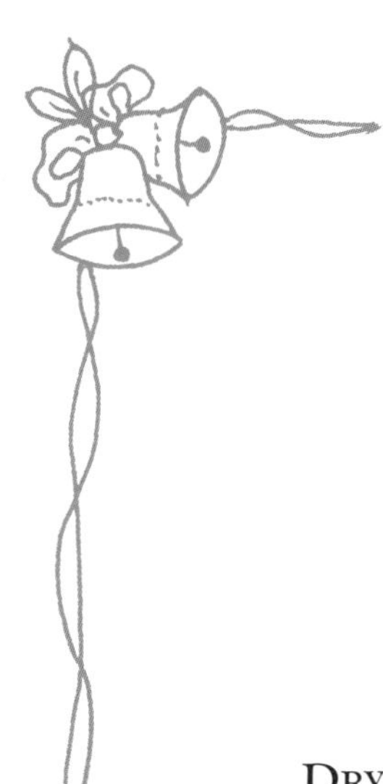

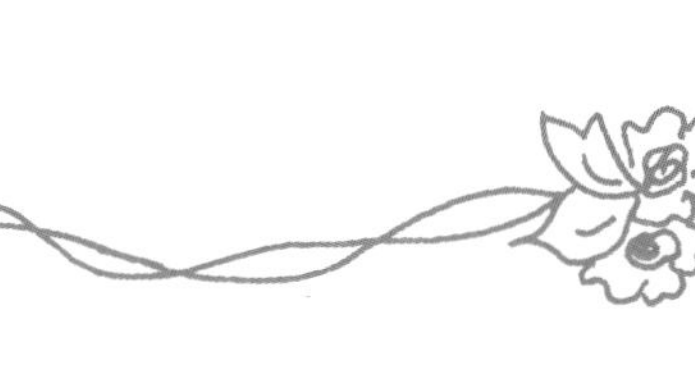

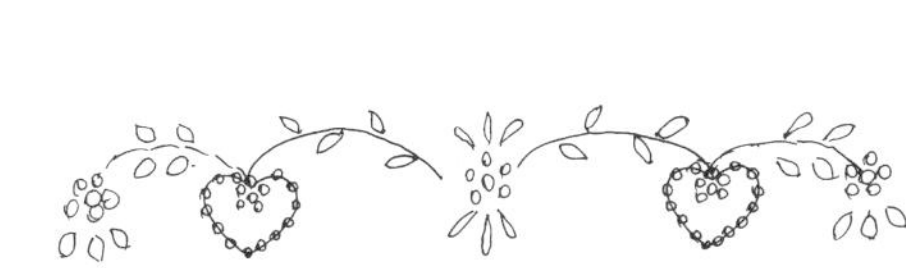

CREATING PAINTED BACKGROUNDS

Faux, or fake, finishes were featured as far back as early Egyptian times. Many timbers and stones were quite expensive, so artists devised ways to copy the real thing. Inlaying timbers and stones was also very time consuming, and it was quicker to mask off areas and paint them.

Today there is a revival of interest in faux finishes and different surface effects. The task is made easier by a variety of mediums, such as Kleister medium, scumbling medium and retarders, and special tools designed to make timber-like grains are available.

These finishes are fascinating to do. Once you have learnt how to do them with simple aids such as a nail brush or sponge, you will be able to create your own effects, or use several different finishes together.

The Blue Lapis Lazuli Pot, the Bride's Bath Box and the Bride's Best Undie Box all feature faux finishes or attractive surface effects and colours.

Sponging

Sponging is used on many items in the book. Colour or colours are applied with a sponge and, depending on the type of sponge and the amount of pressure used, the end result will be a plain basecoat coverage or a decorative textured finish of several colours. Please refer to the Resort Case on page 108, as this will give you a clear picture of what sponging is all about.

You will need disposable gloves, a sponge, a basin of water, a tray for the paint, paint, paper towel, and practice paper. Sponges come in all shapes and sizes for example, household, makeup,

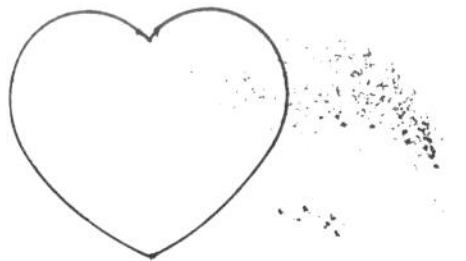

light

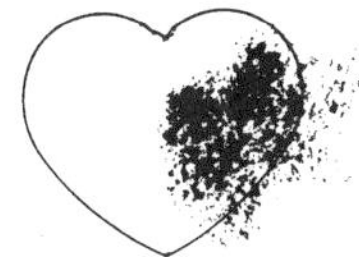

heavy

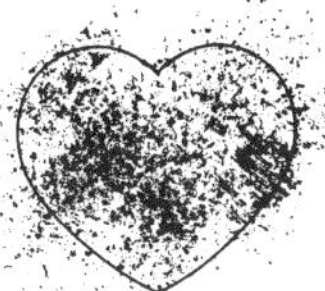

good mixture

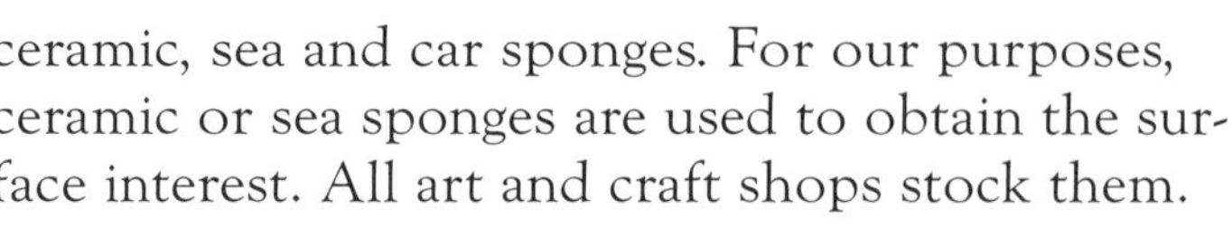

ceramic, sea and car sponges. For our purposes, ceramic or sea sponges are used to obtain the surface interest. All art and craft shops stock them.

1. Please check the instructions for each project. Sometimes a basecoat is applied first.

2. Put on the gloves, dip the sponges in water and squeeze out. Pick up a little of the paint from the tray and dab off any excess on the paper towels. Working a small area at a time, dab lightly in drifts. Turn the sponge, pick up another colour and lightly drift this close to and over the previous colour. Quickly turn the sponge again, pick up more paint and water if needed, and keep dabbing.

   You should have a good coverage by now, but your sponge may be full, so wring out again and repeat the process — more paint, turn the sponge, dab lightly and so on. When you are happy with the different colours, the blending and coverage, move to another spot.

3. When the first sponged layer is dry, you can sponge again, or apply a final light drift here and there with gold or white.

Fantasy Marbling

This technique is shown on the Bride's Bath Box. You will need two colours — one darker for the marbled surface, the other paler for the veining — plastic wrap and a feather.

1. Seal the surface and apply a basecoat. Allow to dry.

2. Apply a thick coat of the darker paint. Scrunch up the plastic wrap, apply it to the wet surface and lift off. Allow to dry.

3. Use a feather to trace fine lines of the lighter diluted colour over the marbled surface. These lines create the impression of veining.

Feather hunting is fun and I have quite a collection. So when out walking in bird country, keep your eyes on the ground.

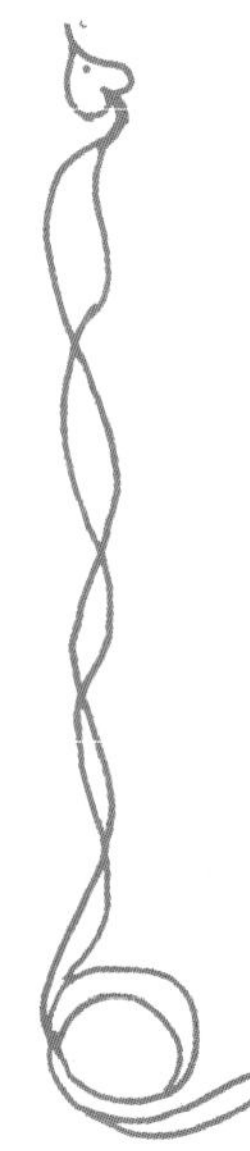

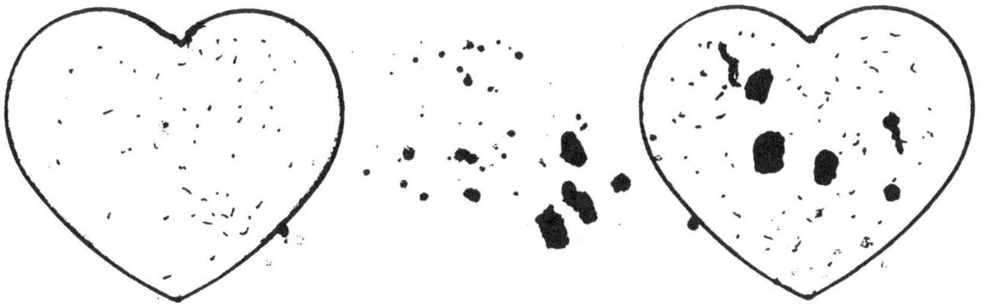

fine mist   blobs   blobs and spatter

Spattering

Spattering is an ageing technique that creates a 'fly-speckled' surface. Use it to make fake speckled stone shown on the Granite Photo Frame, to create a misty look and to add surface interest.

You will need a protected spattering area, disposable gloves, a saucer, water-thinned paint, an old toothbrush, an old paintbrush and paper towels.

1. For a fine mist and spray, load the thinned paint onto the toothbrush, tap off any excess, no drips please, turn the brush down over the area to be sprayed and flick the bristles with your index finger. Stop when you like the effect.

2. For selective spattering, when you don't want the spray to go over certain areas of your work, just mask off these areas with pieces of paper.

3. For blobs, load the old paintbrush, hold it over your work, then tap the brush with another brush. The blobs will fall off — some small, some larger.

A combination of blobs and fine spatter can look great, especially if using different colours, including metallics.

Note: sometimes it is a good idea to varnish the work before spattering. The varnish acts as a barrier, and if a mistake is made, it can be lightly wiped off the varnished surface. (It could not be removed from a painted surface.)

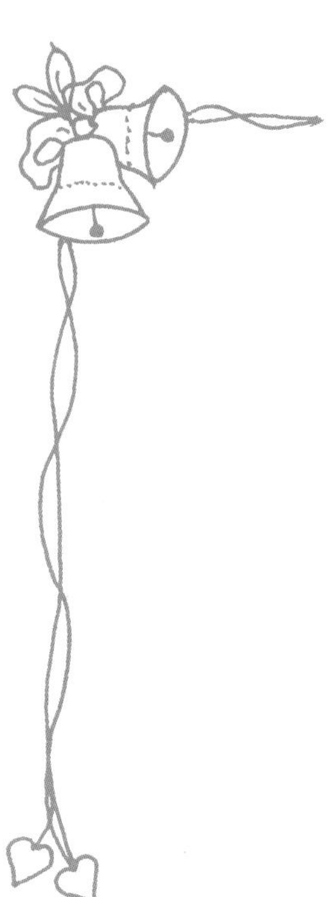

Faux Lapis Lazuli

Lapis Lazuli is a semi-precious stone. The stone was crushed to produce the first blue colour, ultramarine, and crushed stone was used for hundreds of years, until the colour could be manufactured chemically. Artists created faux lapis lazuli finishes in Egyptian times, because the cost of using real semi-precious stones in finishes was too high, even for the wealthy.

This is a lovely finish to do. For full instructions, see the Blue Lapis Lazuli Pot on page 66.

Faux Fabric

This finish was devised to resemble woven check material. A nail brush was dragged across the paint to look like threads. Please refer to the Resort Case colour plate and the instructions on page 108.

Gold Leafing

The application of gold leaf adds a richness and lustre to any item. It can be applied to many surfaces including leather, paper and timber. Today we see gold-leafed fruit, papier-mâché boxes, stars, cherubs and lettering.

I have an old small table that is entirely gold-leafed. The top has been painted with black, and over that there is a beautifully painted spray of flowers. The whole table has been antiqued. It is a treasure, and even though it looks worn and used and scratched in places, the workmanship is a delight. Your pieces too will become treasures. So while painting with Rich or Pale Gold is an alternative, why not try gold leafing and learn a very old craft?

Traditional techniques use real gold, beaten to a thin sheet, but today we use a composite metal leaf called Dutch Metal, which comes in gold, silver and copper. The extremely fine foil-like leaf comes in small sheets, with waxed paper between each sheet.

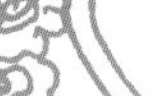

The waxed paper makes the sheets easier to handle and cut, allowing you to pick up the leaf without your fingers touching it. The perspiration from your hands affects the leaf, tarnishing the gold. As an extra precaution, always wear cotton gloves when handling the leaf.

To gold leaf, you will need Burgundy or Napthol Crimson, a paintbrush, tannin blocking sealer, cotton or disposable gloves, scissors, sheets or block of Dutch Metal, cotton balls and a glass of hot water and soap.

1. Decide where you want the gold leaf to go, then apply one coat of Burgundy or Napthol Crimson within this area. The leaf is supposed to glow better with this undercoat. If any small veins appear in the gold leaf, this colour will show through. Note that the cherub on the Antiqued Gold Leaf Cherub Gift Box is not given any undercoat, because it will be antiqued and any little cracks will take on a dark colour anyway.

2. Apply two coats of the tannin blocking sealer, which acts as a glue. The gold leaf can be applied when it is at the tacky stage. The leaf will adhere only where the sealer is. The rest peels away when dry. So it is a matter of painting only where you want the leaf to go. Apply the sealer evenly, as any ridges will show under the leaf.

3. Put on the gloves and cut leaf to size, tearing it off the pad and keeping the wax paper together with the gold leaf. It is not a good idea to stand in a draught, to breathe heavily or sneeze at this stage.

4. Gently place the leaf and wax paper down over the glue, allowing some overlap. Gently press the leaf in place. For covering the grooves, more than one layer of leaf may be needed. This is so on the Old Silver Frame. The left-over leaf should be saved for this purpose.

5. Gently rub the surface of the wax paper round and round. You can almost feel the gold leaf

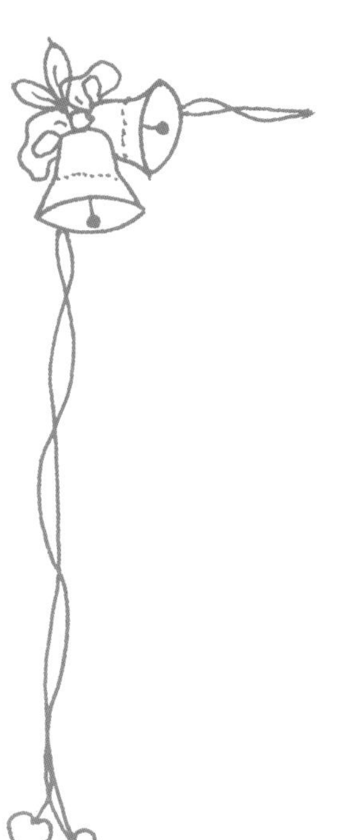

sticking. A hair dryer will assist the drying process; otherwise, leave to dry overnight.

6. In the morning dip a cotton ball into the soap and hot water, squeeze out and rub gently over the leaf. The excess leaf will come away, leaving the outline and the leaf firmly in place. Repeat the process if a spot has been missed.

7. Once it is dry, gold leaf can be sealed, painted, antiqued and varnished.

Silver Leafing

Silver leaf is used for the Old Silver Frame. The method is the same as for gold leaf. Rather than undercoating with Burgundy or Napthol Crimson, apply a coat of Ultramarine Blue, as this is supposed to make the silver glow. Allow extra silver to get into all the grooves made by the cord and plastic shapes. Refer to the Old Silver Frame colour plate.

Backgrounds and Finishes

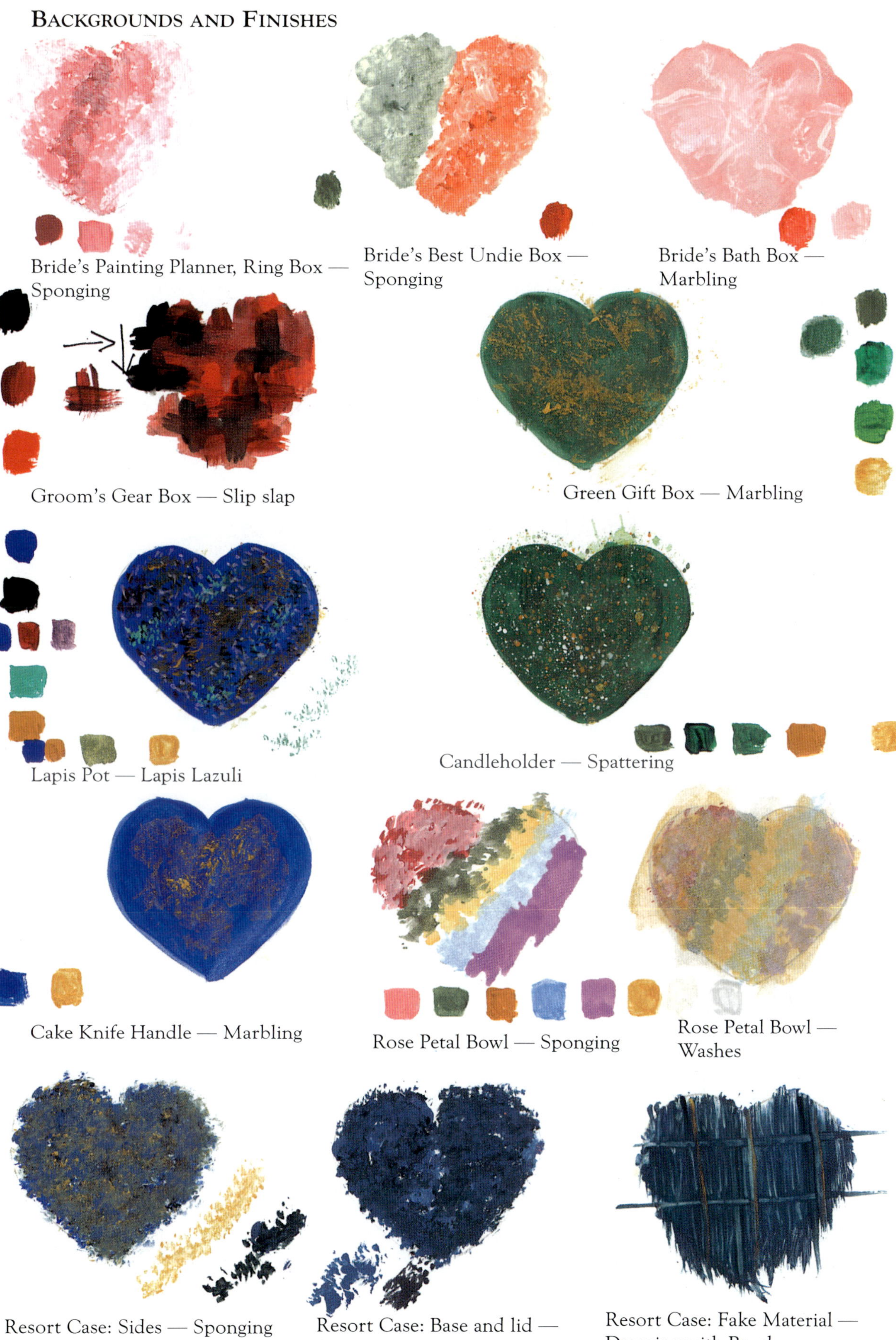

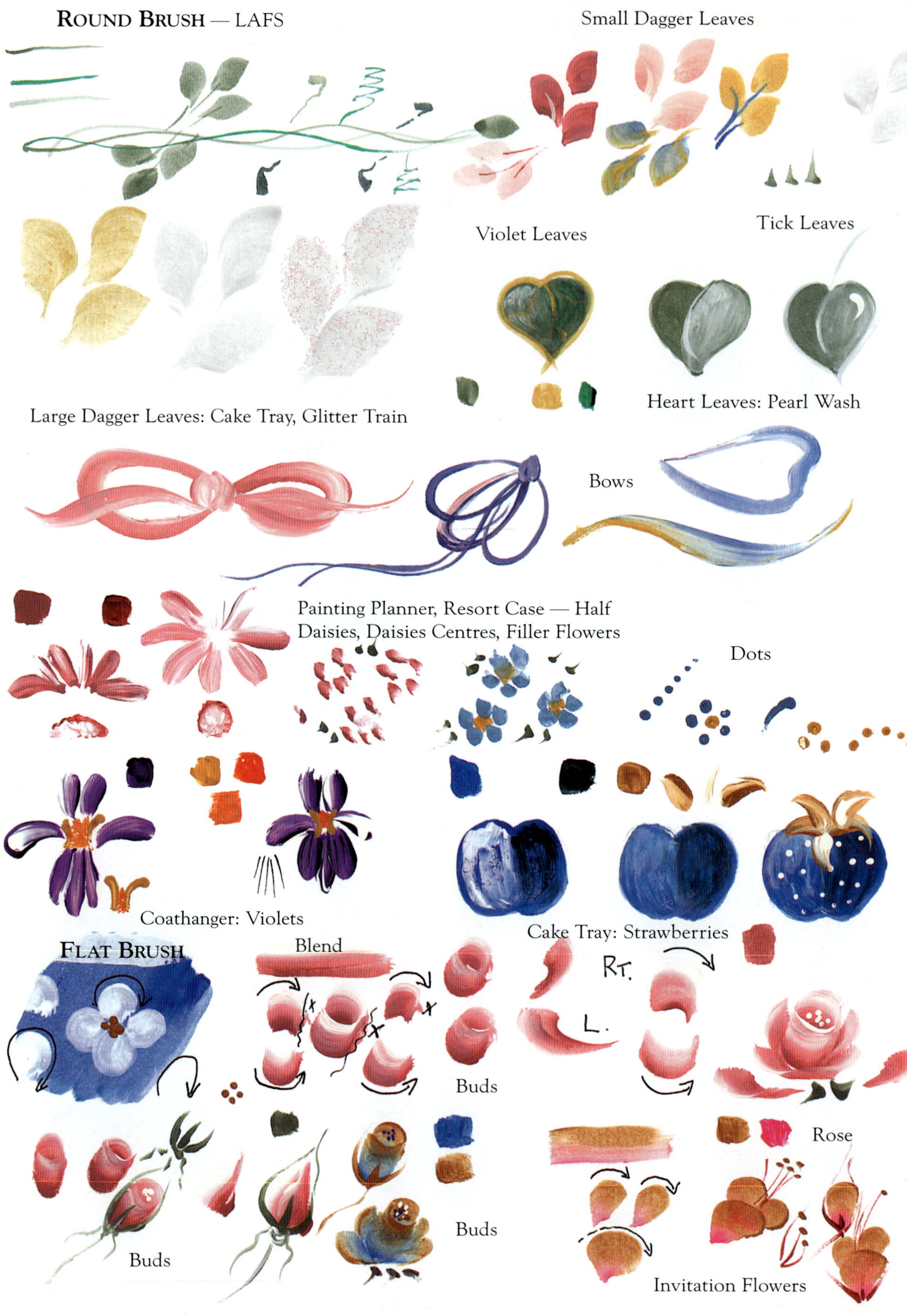

Round Brush — LAFS
Small Dagger Leaves
Violet Leaves
Tick Leaves
Large Dagger Leaves: Cake Tray, Glitter Train
Heart Leaves: Pearl Wash
Bows
Painting Planner, Resort Case — Half
Daisies, Daisies Centres, Filler Flowers
Dots
Coathanger: Violets
Cake Tray: Strawberries
Flat Brush
Blend
RT.
L.
Buds
Buds
Buds
Rose
Buds
Invitation Flowers

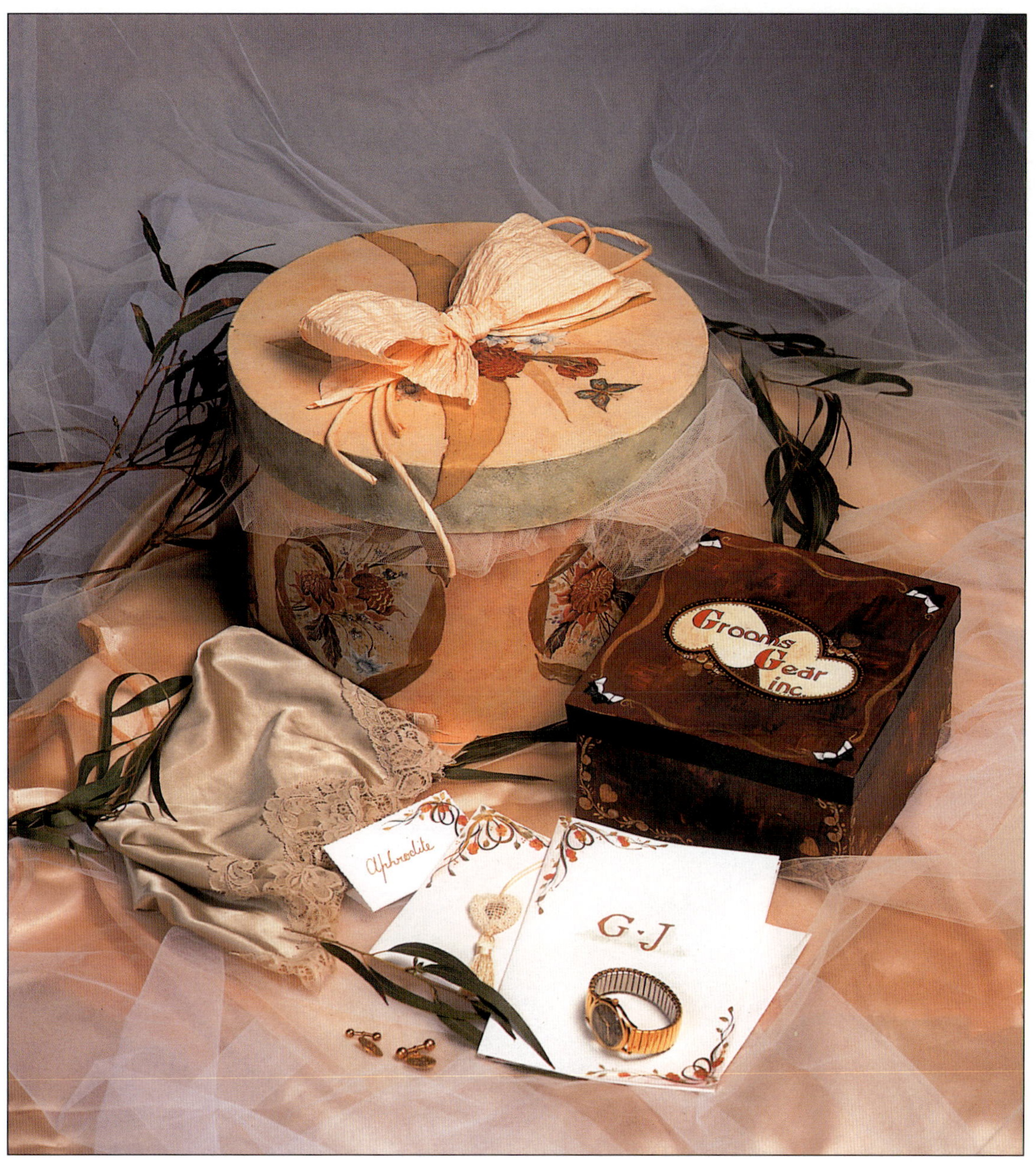

BRIDE'S BEST UNDIE BOX, GROOM'S GEAR BOX, WEDDING INVITATIONS AND PLACE CARDS.

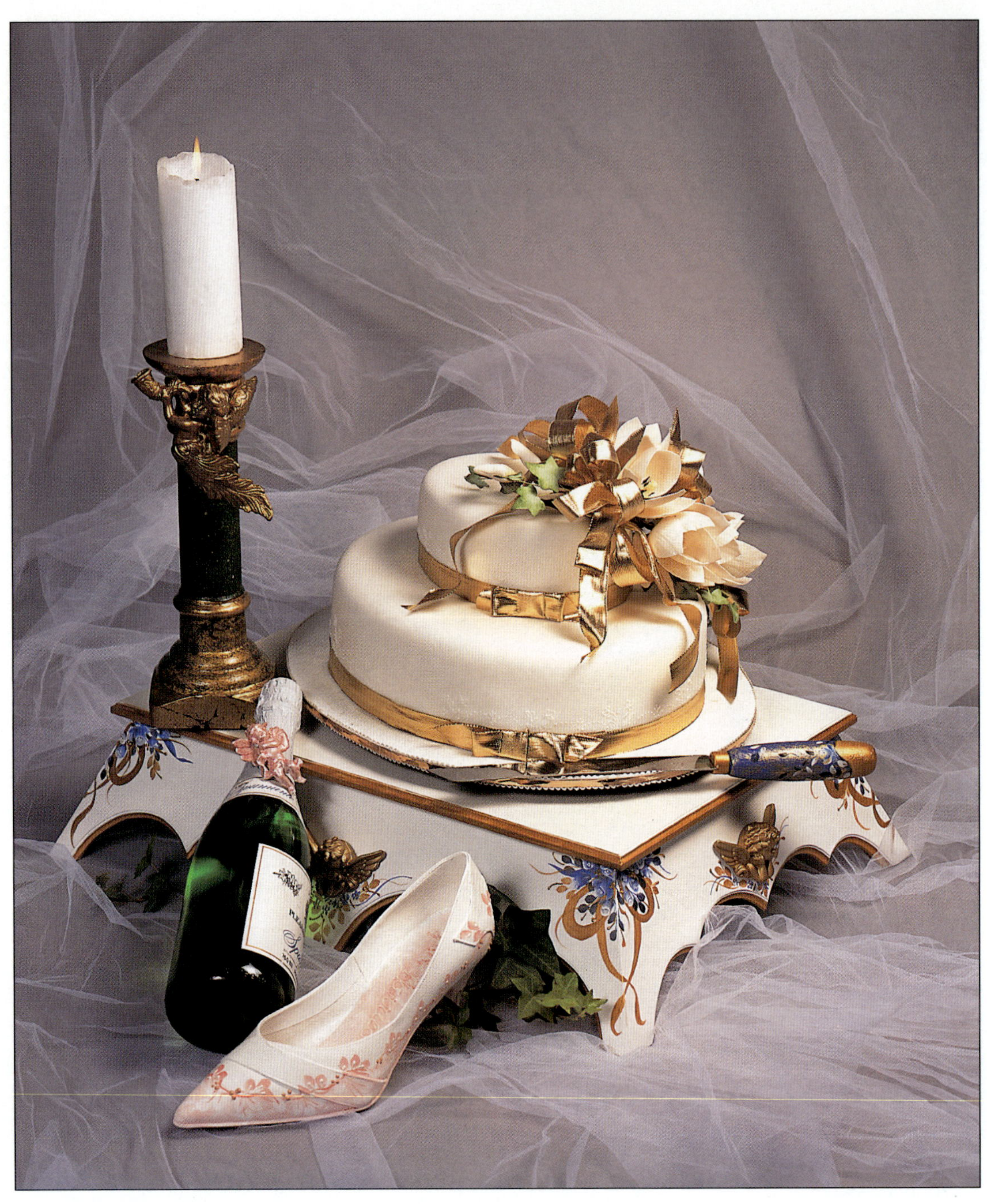

GOLD LEAF CANDLEHOLDER, CAKE STAND, PINK CHAMPAGNE SLIPPER AND
GRANNY'S OLD CHINA KNIFE.

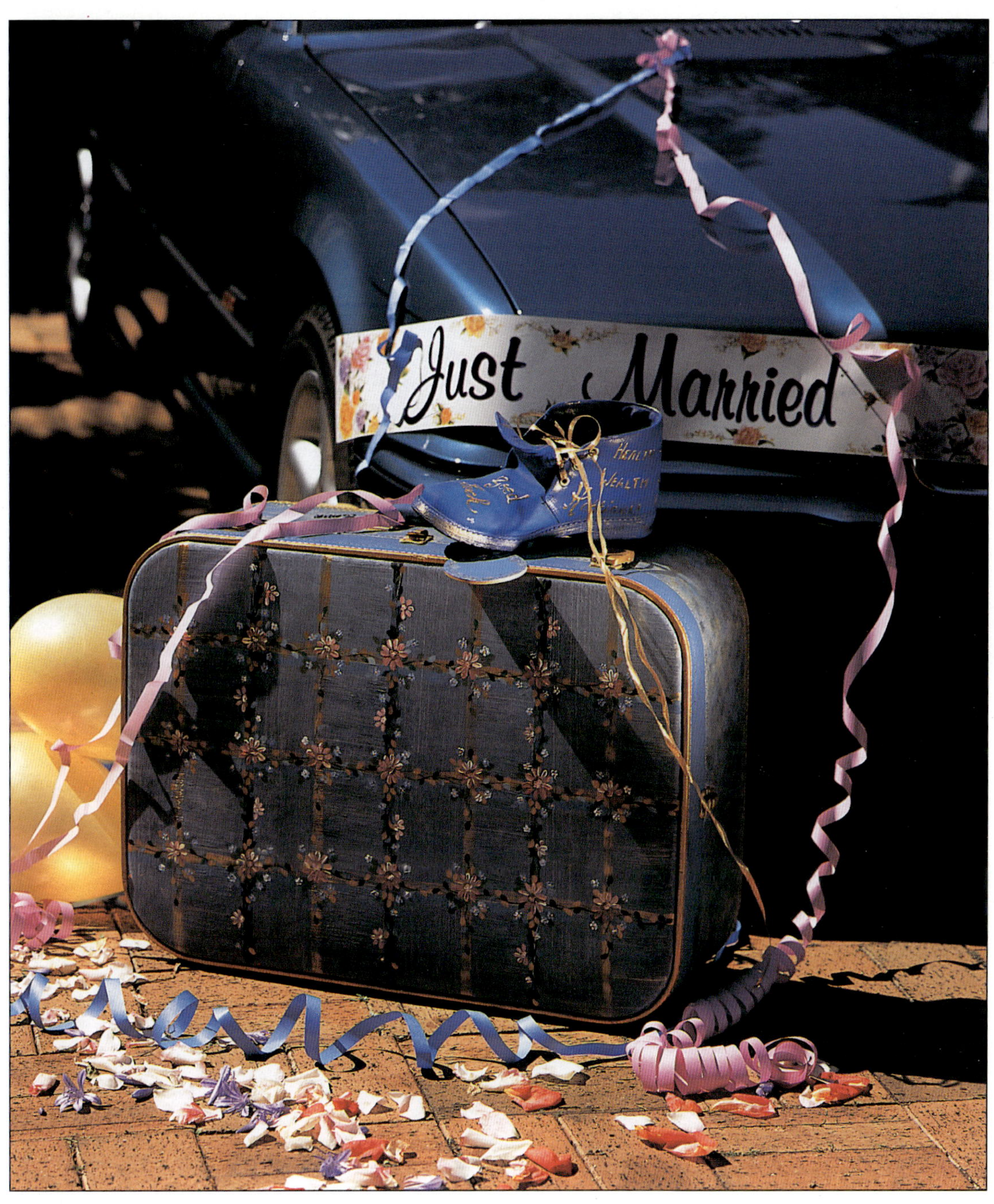

RESORT CASE AND LUCKY BOOT.

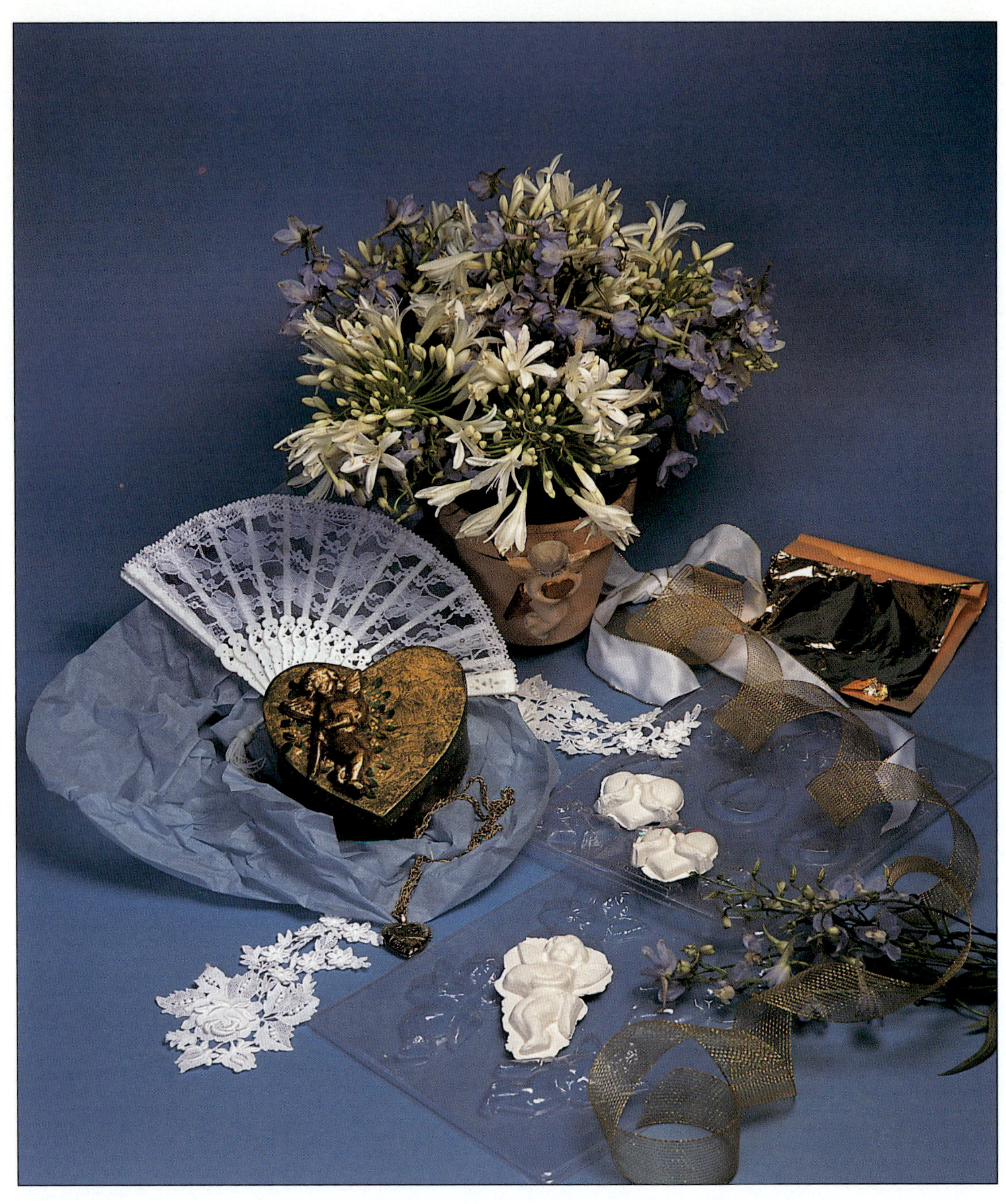

Antique Gold Leaf Cherub Gift Box, Peach and Gold Cherub Pot.

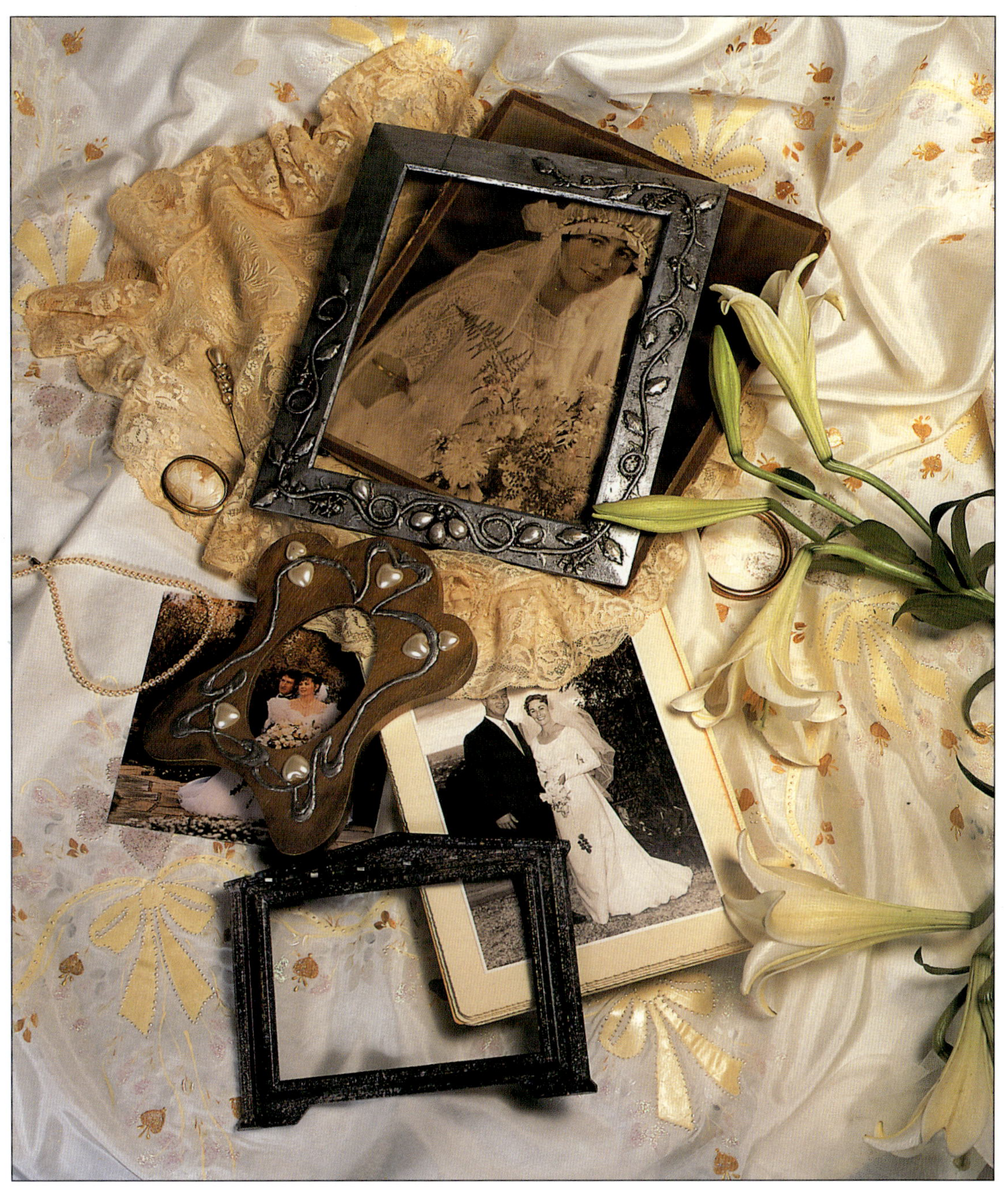

OLD SILVER FRAME, GOLD, PEARL AND PEWTER FRAME, GRANITE PHOTO FRAME, WITH BRIDAL TRAIN IN BACKGROUND.

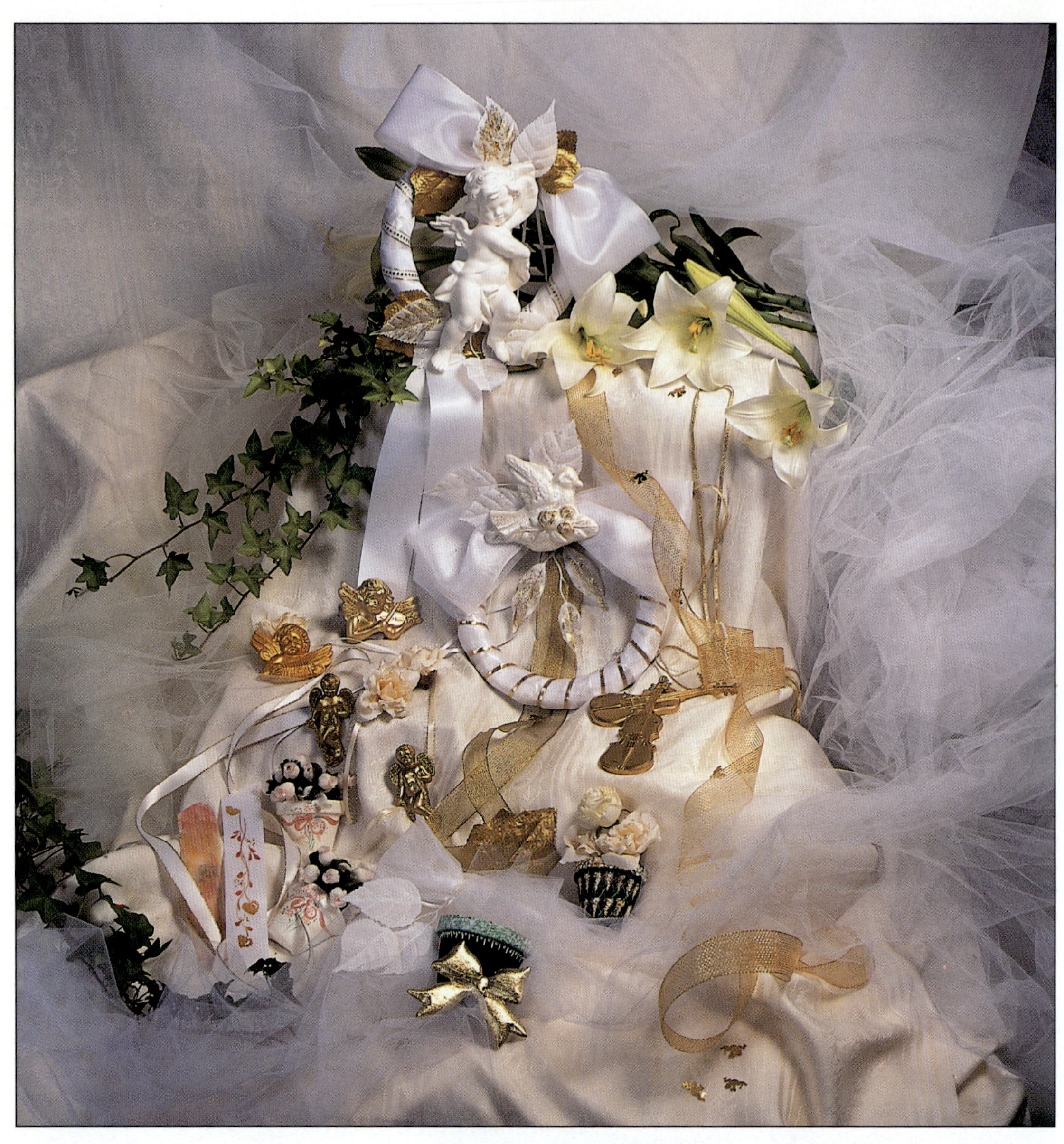

WHITE BISQUE HALF POTS AND GREEN HALF POTS FOR PEWS: SPONGED
POTS AND WISTERIA POTS.

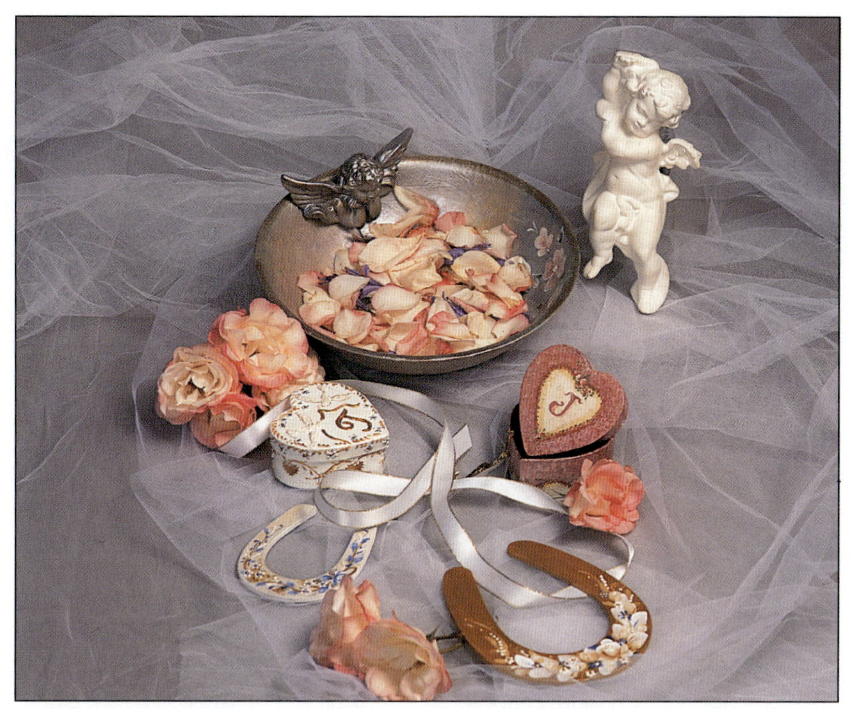

ABOVE: RAINBOW RICE OR ROSE PETAL BOWL, HEARTS AND DOVES RING BOX, PINK HEART RING OR CUFFS BOX, LUCKY HORSESHOES.

BELOW: BRIDAL TRAIN WITH SHOES TO MATCH.

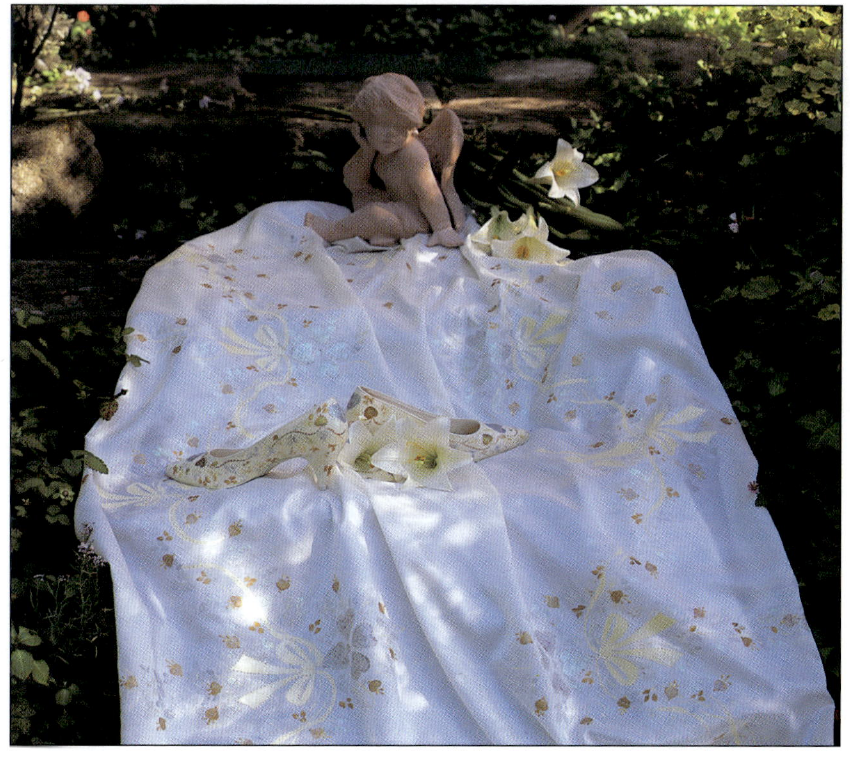

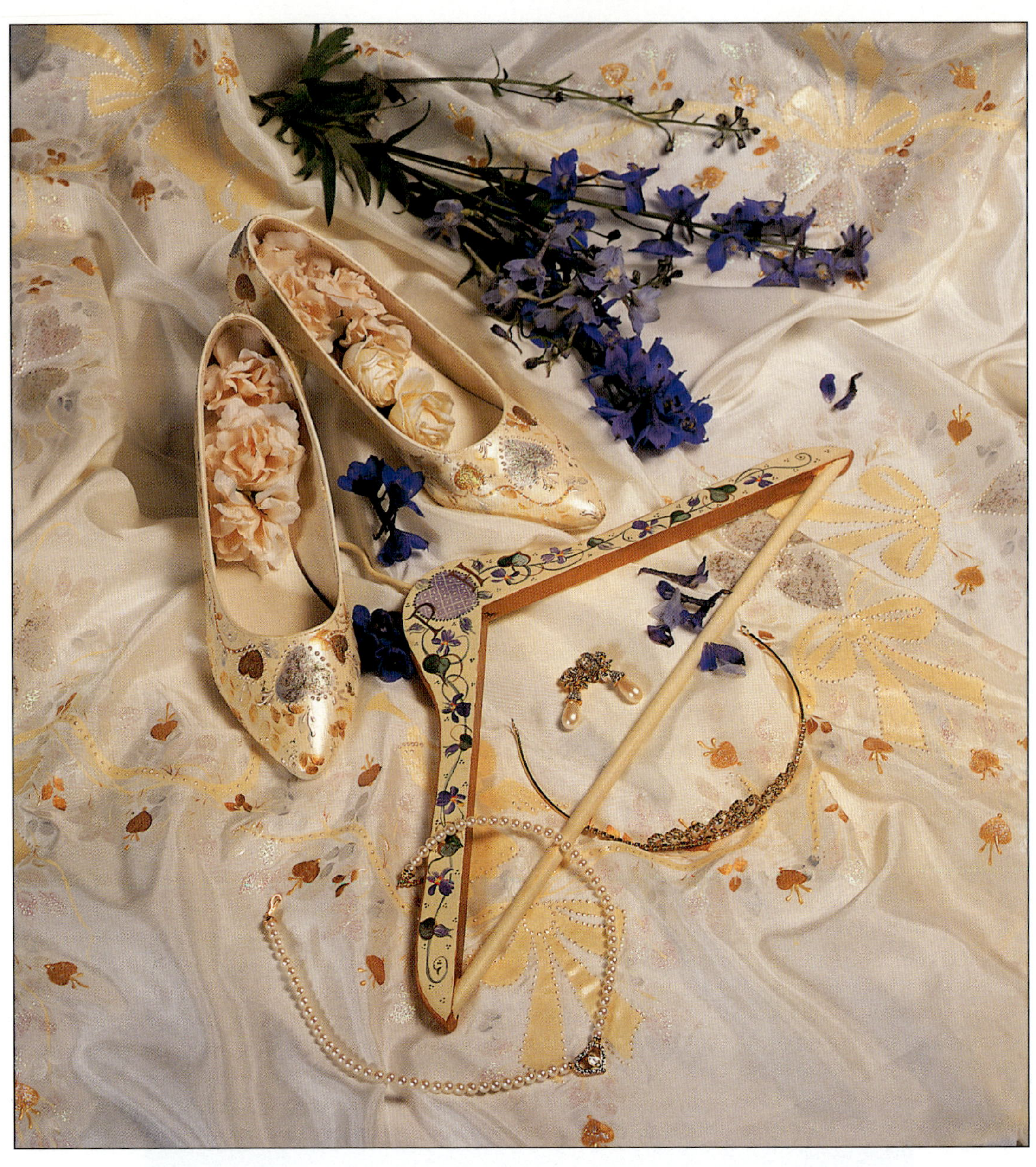

Coat Hanger, Bridal Train and Shoes to Match Bridal Train

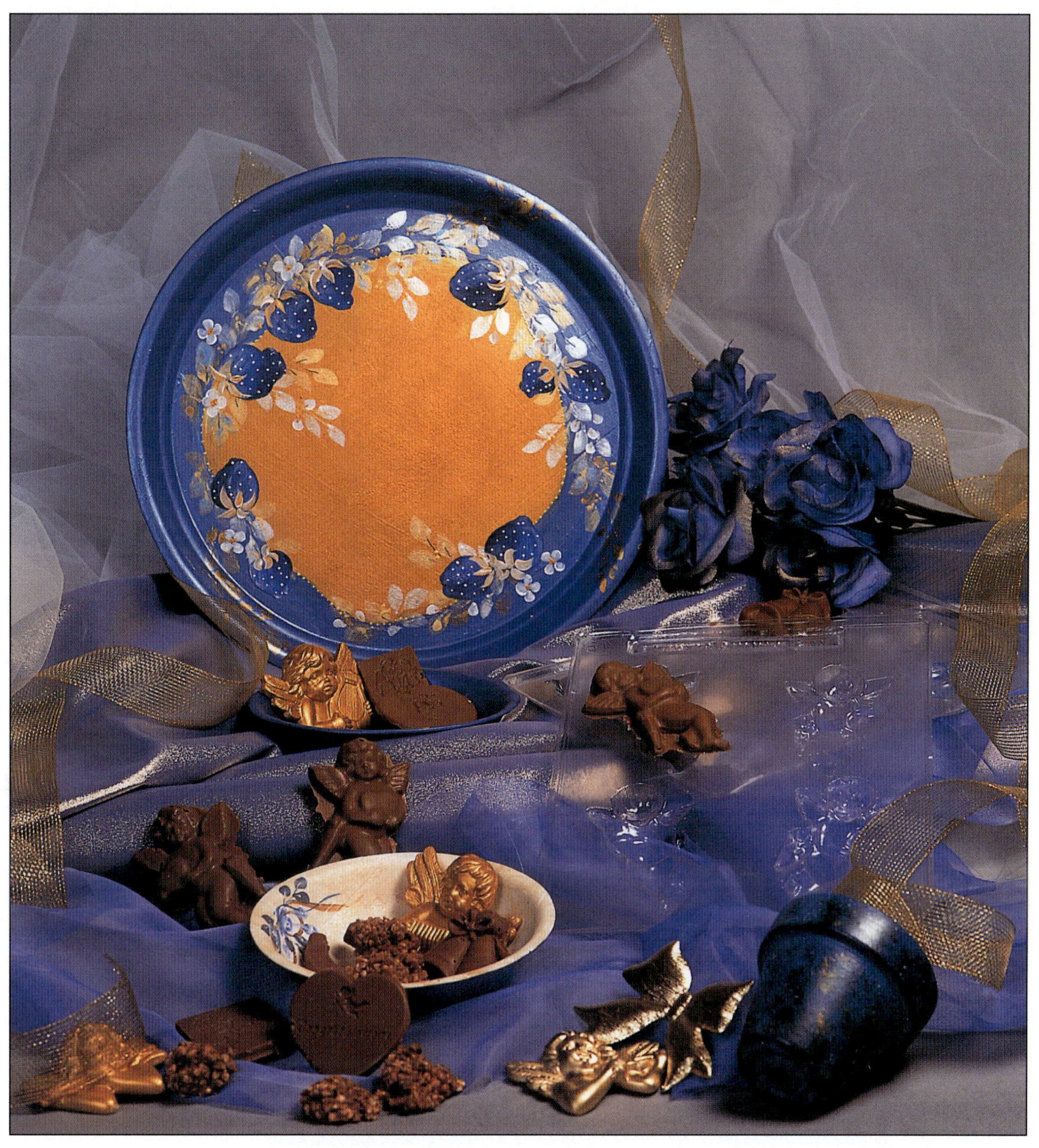

Blue and Gold Strawberry Cake Tray, Painted Chocolate Bowls, Lapis Lazuli Blue Sponged Pot.

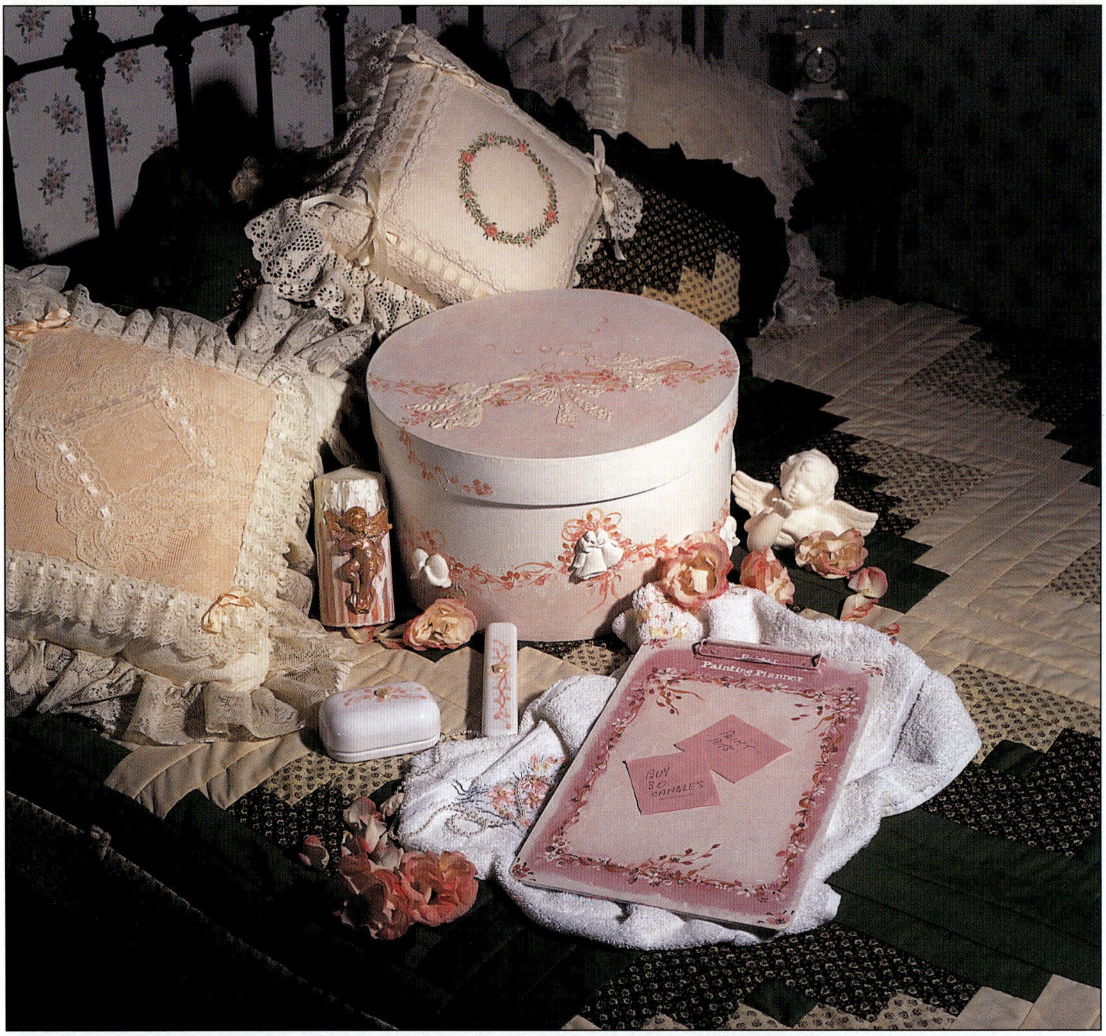

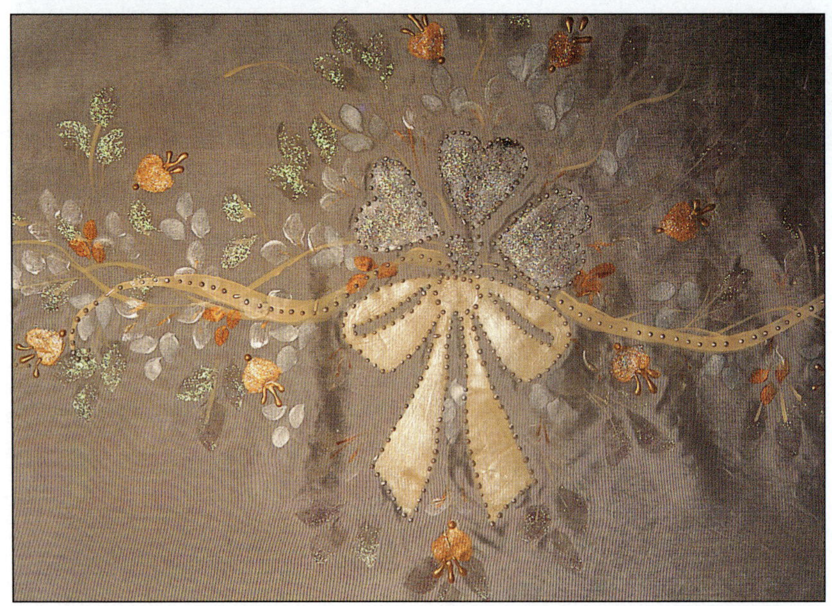

ABOVE: BRIDE'S
PANTRY
PLANNER,
BRIDE'S BATH
BOX.

LEFT: DETAIL OF
PAINTED TRAIN.

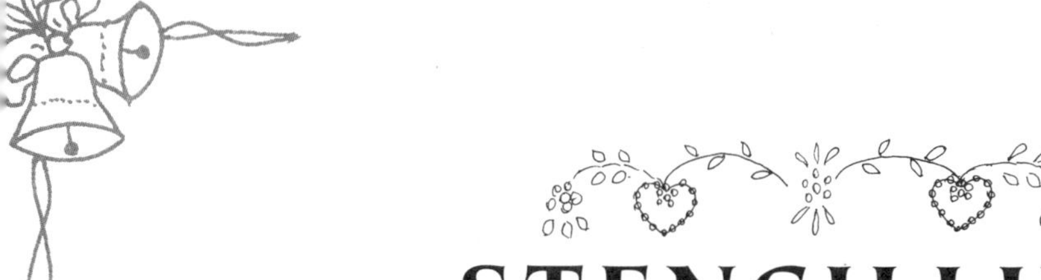

STENCILLING AND TEMPLATES

Stencilling

Stencilling is an age-old craft, which is very popular today. Folk painters can use stencilling as a quick way to basecoat shapes. For example, the dozens of little hearts on the Painted Train were stencilled with gold. Stencils are also useful for lettering, and alphabet stencils come in all types — Early Roman, Gothic, Victorian and Art Deco, just for starters.

Modern production and cutting techniques are used to produce metal, plastic or paper stencils, and sheets of cut-out shapes and letters. The more complex and delicate stencil designs are usually made from brass sheeting. Stencils are found in most art and craft shops, as well as in toy shops and supermarkets. I have quite a large collection.

For stencilling, you will need a stencil brush, which has bristles that are quite stiff and short. Alternatively, the cheap Chinese brushes with pig bristles are quite adequate when they are cut short.

1. Press the edges of the stencil down as you apply the paint to prevent the paint from bleeding underneath the stencil. Lift the stencil off carefully.

2. If two coats are needed, it is easier to paint the second coat with a round brush, once the stencil shape has been established.

In order to preserve the edges of paper stencils, I usually paint them with one or two coats of sealer. The paint can then be wiped off, and the stencils last longer. All stencils should be checked and wiped before using again. Plastic stencils can be washed in warm detergent and hung to dry. Store flat in a folder.

Templates

Templates are an easy way to create positive and negative shapes. Borders painted around a cut-out and sponged shape look great on the lids of boxes. To make a template, you will need a sheet of A4 paper, a fine-point pen, scissors and Magic Tape.

1. Fold the sheet of A4 paper in halves. Transfer the outline of the centre shape onto the folded paper. (You will only need to transfer a half of the design.)

2. Cut out the shape carefully. Do not discard the cut-out shape.

3. Tape the template to the painting surface using Magic Tape. You can now paint the shape with a single colour, like a basecoat, or sponge with several colours. Press the edges of the paper down when you sponge to prevent bleeding.

4. You can use both parts of the template, as in the Bride's Painting Planner. Once the sponged or painted shape in the centre of the paper is dry, place the cut-out shape on this shape to match, and sponge or paint the area outside with different colours.

TEMPLATES

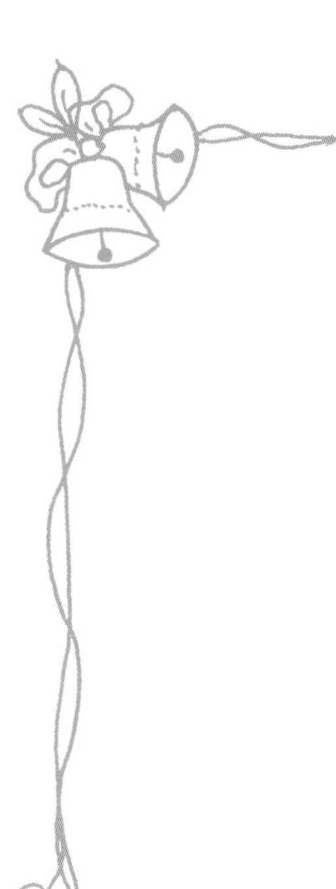
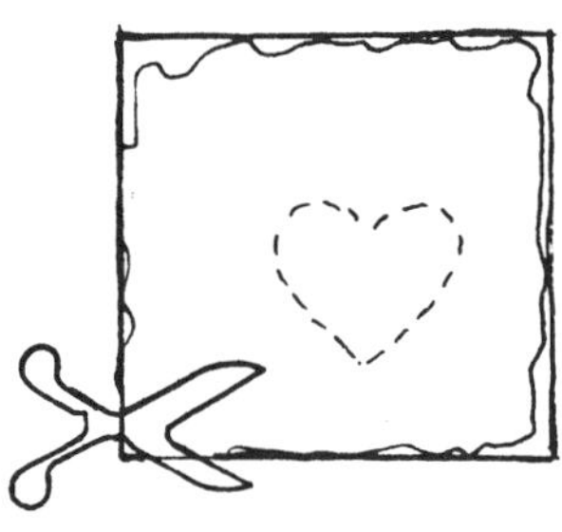
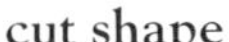

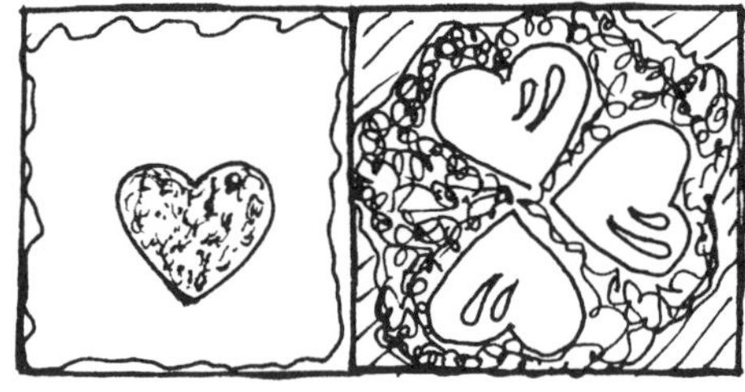

cut shape keep shape positive and negative designs

Note: once a template has been cut it actually becomes a stencil but has positive and negative shapes

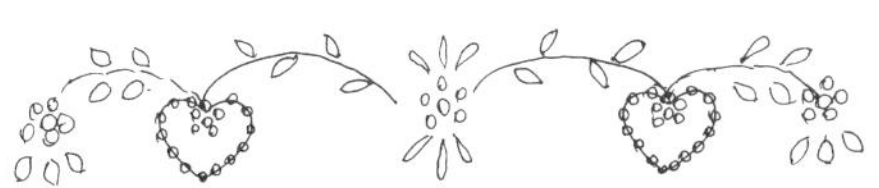

TRACING THE DESIGN

Keep tracings of original designs in a manilla folder for future use, and include any notes made during the painting such as the colours used.

For tracing, you will need a fine-point pen, greaseproof paper, Magic Tape and graphite paper or Saral paper, which comes in several colours. I use white graphite paper for darker backgrounds and blue or grey for the lighter backgrounds. You will also need a stylus or satay stick and a kneadable eraser.

1. Depending on the size of the item you are working on, you may need to enlarge or reduce the design provided on a photocopier.

2. Using the fine-point pen, trace the design carefully onto greaseproof paper. Position the design on the piece you are going to paint. Secure with Magic Tape if necessary.

3. Slide a sheet a graphite paper under the tracing, with the graphite side towards the surface.

4. Lightly trace the outline with the metal point of the stylus or a satay stick. Please note that if you are using a design enlarged on a photocopier, you may need to press harder, because the paper is thicker. Lift and check from time to time. There is no need to transfer fine details, such as the veins in leaves or facial features, because these will be basecoated over anyway. They can be retraced after basecoating. The fewer lines the better. When the painting is complete, use a kneadable eraser to rub out any remaining lines.

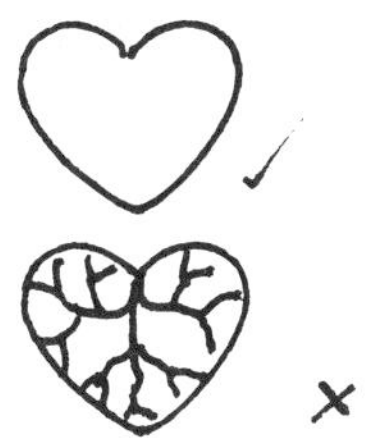

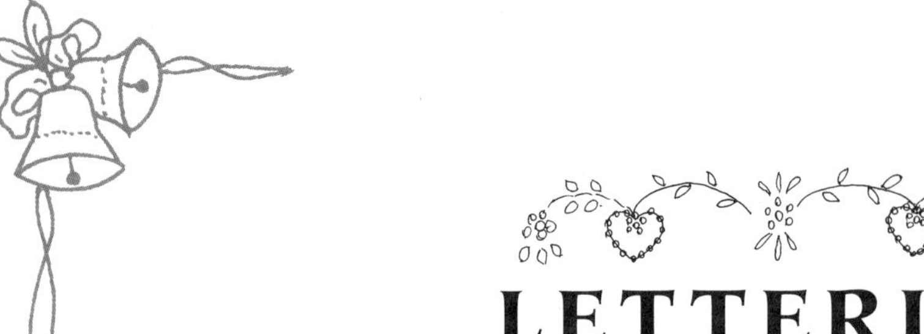

LETTERING

Letters and initials need to be measured, drawn onto paper with a fine-point pencil or pen, enlarged or reduced on a photocopier, then traced onto the piece. Or you can use one of the many alphabet stencils available (see Stencilling on page 33). If you are fortunate enough to have good handwriting or you have studied calligraphy, you can do freehand lettering on the piece with a carbothello pencil or a pen and paint over the top.

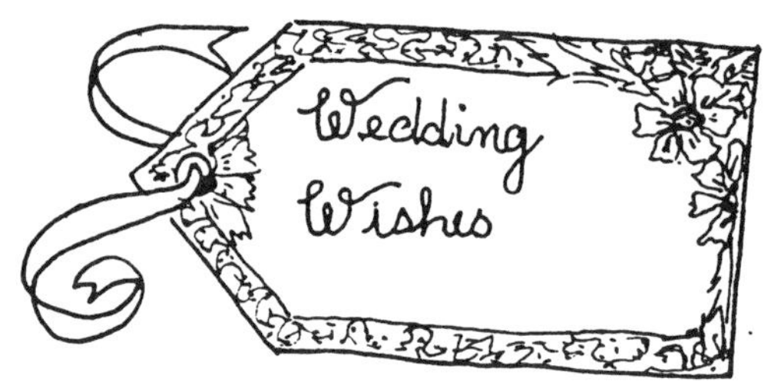

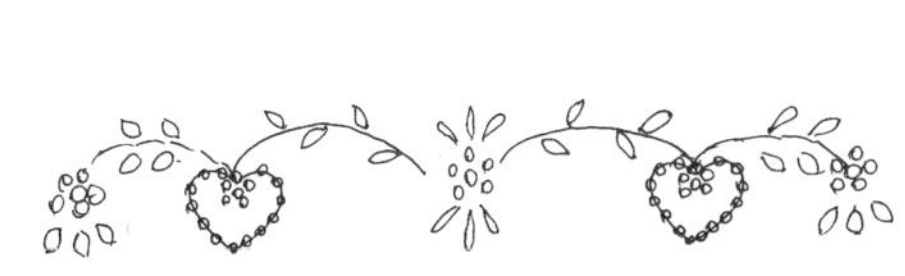

USING MOULDS

There are many different moulds available, which can be used for both DAS and chocolate shapes. Have a look in cake decorating shops.

DAS Cherubs and Wedding Shapes

DAS is a compound that air-dries hard. It is inexpensive, goes a long way and can be sanded and painted. It has a lot of craft possibilities. DAS is available from art suppliers. It can be hand-moulded, but I was happy with the shapes made in the moulds. Please read the instructions on the packet.

1. Work DAS with a little water and press into mould.
2. Remove the shapes from the moulds before they dry, and let them dry flat.
3. When dry, sand the backs and edges, paint as directed and glue onto the pots or boxes with craft glue.

Note: Because the Bride's Bath Box is round, remove the DAS from the moulds while damp, and curve the shapes so that they fit around the circle. If you forget, you can fill the gaps with more DAS after you have glued the shapes on. Make small balls of DAS, and pack them in the gaps with a toothpick.

Chocolate Cherubs and Wedding Shapes

Handmade chocolates are divine to eat and fun to make. You can mix a diverse range of ingredients

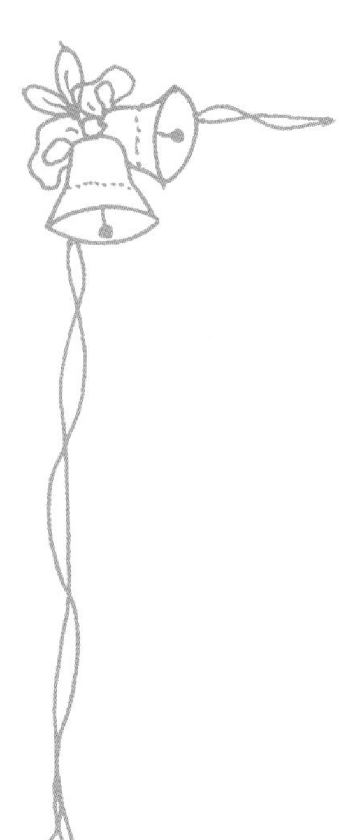

with the chocolate, and you can use milk, dark, or white chocolate.

A double boiler is the best way to melt the chocolate. Spoon the melted chocolate mixture into the moulds (wash them before using them) or onto foil, then set in the refrigerator for a short time. The chocolates can be stored between greaseproof paper in tins in a cool place for several months. Naturally, the chocolates needed to be tasted from time to time, and there were lots of offers to lick the spoon and basin. My son-in-law became an expert at making them.

Here are some delicious ideas for mixing chocolates:

- Add chopped apricots to the melted chocolate, dip whole apricots in chocolate or put chocolate on top of the whole fruit with a walnut on top.

- Add chopped nuts, whole nuts, slivered or crushed nuts — use almonds, walnuts, macadamia nuts, peanuts, hazelnuts or pecans.

- Add coconut, shaved and shredded, to the chocolate.

- Use liqueurs or essences to flavour.

- Swirl the different-coloured chocolates together.

- Shave hard chocolate into the melted chocolate.

- Roll the chocolate in nuts.

- Add dried fruits and toasted seeds such as sunflower and sesame.

- Crumble biscuits, caramel, toffee or Violet Crumble into the chocolate.

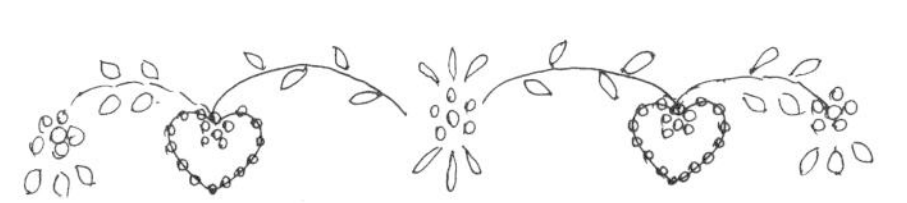

FINISHING TECHNIQUES

All items need a final protective coat of varnish. Some of the items in this book have also been antiqued, giving them a subtly aged appearance.

Antiquing

Antiquing is a method of deliberately ageing a painted piece, whether it be wood, metal, canvas or paper. Antiquing also softens harsh lines, emphasises outlines and creates shadows. Sometimes the antiquing mixture is left on the article for a long period and then only a little is wiped off. This is called mudding. For a wedding, I prefer a softer, more subtle look.

The pieces antiqued in this book are the Gold Leaf Cherub, The Old Silver Frame and the fake pewter on the Gold, Pearl and Pewter Frame.

To antique these items, you will need a water-based varnish, Burnt Umber, Turner's Yellow, Jo Sonja's Retarder and Antiquing Medium, an old brush, a soft cloth (like very old sheeting) and cotton buds.

1. Make sure the article to be antiqued is very dry, then apply a coat of water-based varnish.

2. Make a mix of Burnt Umber, a tiny amount of Turner's Yellow and some Retarder and Antiquing Medium. Aim to make a mix that is thinnish, but not too watery. Brush this over the article, covering all your beautiful work in a muddy colour. The medium slows down the drying time of the paint, so you have a lot of time to play around with.

3. Allow to stand for about an hour, then very gen-

tly remove the Burnt Umber mix with a very soft cloth. Wipe firmly where you want the painting revealed but do not wipe too hard where you want the antiquing mixture to remain. For example, for the Gold Leaf Cherub on the gift box, leave more of the antiquing mixture in the grooves. For the cherub, remove more of the antiquing medium from the tummy, the quiver, the hair and the arms and legs.

When removing the medium from confined places, use a cotton bud to get in. If you remove too much medium, you can wipe some more on.

When thoroughly dry, varnish the article with at least two coats.

When you become more familiar with antiquing, and really get into folk painting, mix a larger quantity of the antiquing mixture and store in a jar. The mixture lasts for a long time. Other colours such as black, dark blue, burgundy and dark green can also be used.

Varnishing

Varnishing gives the final touch to a painted piece, as well as protecting the painted surface.

Depending on the required finish, such as hard, light, gloss or semi-gloss, and the usage the piece will receive, there are several varnishes to choose from:

Jo Sonja's water-based varnish (This is ideal for folk painting.)

Intergrain (This is a water-based stronger type of varnish, which can be obtained from paint shops.) — my favourite varnish.

Derivan (This is a polymer gloss varnish. Used on paper, it acts as a glue as well as a coating. I do not use this over my folk painting.) This varnish comes in 500ml bottles and goes a long way. It was used as a glue and varnish on the Bride's Best Undies Box.

Folk Art spray varnish (I only use this occasionally

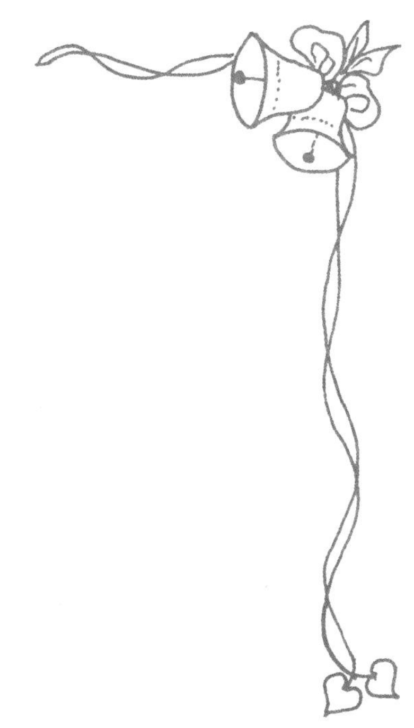

for waterproofing. It is used on the Cake Stand and on the bottom of the Bride's Bath Box.)

To varnish, you will need the best large, fine synthetic brush you can afford or a ceramic sponge, and disposable gloves.

The sponges and brushes wash out in water. Please read all labels thoroughly.

1. Stir the tinned varnish slowly with a flat knife.

2. Apply the varnish with even light strokes, one coat in one direction and the next coat in the opposite direction.

3. Hold the article up to the light and tilt to see if you have missed any spots. A light rub with some wet and dry sandpaper dipped in water will make the surface smooth and get rid of any runs.

4. For spray varnish, please read instructions on can.

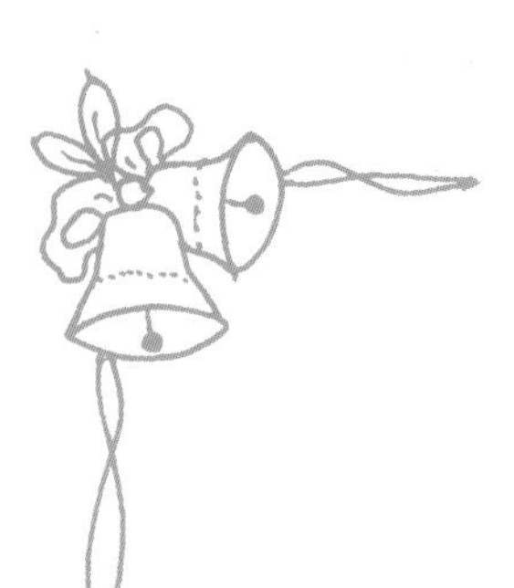

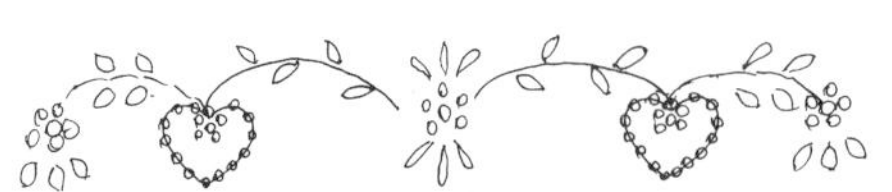

PROJECTS

Bride's Painting Planner

Just as embroidery samplers show the various stitches, this clipboard is a painting 'sampler' that shows the various painting techniques. By the time you have finished this sampler, you will be well on your way to being able to paint most of the projects in this book, and you will understand many of the techniques and the vocabulary of folk art. The completed painted board will also be most useful. Stick on notes to remind yourself of the hundred and one things to be done and purchased.

Before starting to paint, it is a good idea to read through all the information about techniques, paints and brushes. Make a shopping list of all the materials and equipment needed.

If pink, white and gold are not your colours, please choose others.

TECHNIQUES
Templates, sponging, LAFS, dagger leaves, dots, filler flowers, tick leaves

COLOURS
Titanium White, Plum Pink, Rich Gold

BRUSHES
Sponge basecoater, fine liner, ⅛" dagger, No.3 round, ⅛" flat

OTHER MATERIALS
Clipboard, sheet of A4 paper, scissors, Magic Tape, small sea or ceramic sponge, practice paper, stylus or satay stick or toothpick, greaseproof paper for blending, tracing equipment (see page 35, and use grey graphite paper), water-based varnish.

PREPARATION

1. Sand and seal both sides of the clipboard.

2. If the clipboard has a metal clip, wipe it over with equal parts of water and vinegar to make it rustproof, then seal it. Dry around the metal clip with a hair dryer when painting and sponging, and to prevent the clip sticking to the board, place a small piece of plastic under the clip, especially when varnishing..

METHOD

1. Basecoat both sides with at least two coats of Titanium White.

2. As my board was a foolscap size, I cut a template, or pattern, with a scalloped edge from a sheet of A4 paper. (refer to Templates on page 34.) Stick the outside edge of the paper template onto the board with Magic Tape.

3. Sponge in the centre of the template with a pale pink mix of Plum Pink and Titanium White.

4. When dry, place the cut-out centre of the template over this sponged area, and sponge around this shape with a deeper mix of Plum Pink and Titanium White, and more Titanium White. Leave a small outside border of White, the original basecoat colour.

5. Set out the Titanium White and Plum Pink on your palette. Mix a darker pink than the border one, and paint some LAFS trails around the template edge, at the bottom and each top corner. The back of the board can be used as a practice area. Refer to LAFS colour plate.

6. Using the same colour and your ⅛" dagger brush, paint some leaves, placing them mostly on the white edge. (Refer to Dagger Leaves on page 22).

7. With Titanium White and the dagger brush, paint some dagger leaves on the pink area. Paint small veins on the leaves — white on the pink and pink on the white.

8. Paint a few ribbon trails with the dagger brush.

Practise these. If you wish to make loops and bows, you will have to turn the board at an angle so that you have plenty of space to move your arm around in a circle. Using the round or liner brush paint the top of the bow with pressure, turn and release the pressure, ending in a fine line. Repeat for the other side of the bow and make a knot with two small strokes. As these require lots of practice to paint, just paint the trails of ribbons here and there. Add a little Rich Gold to your brush and make some pink and gold ribbons. Clean the brush.

9. Load your No.3 round brush with Plum Pink, pick up some white paint on the tip of the brush and paint some five- or six-petalled daisies. Reload the brush for each petal. Paint a few half daisies in a gap. For the centres of the daisies, use the end of the stylus to place dots of White in a circle, then dots of Plum Pink in part of the centre to look like a shadow. Reverse this shadow on some of the centres. Clean the brush.

10. Painting the buds and small roses requires prac-tice too. (Refer to Flat Brush Blending on page 21).Blend the paint on the flat brush and place the brush's chisel edge on the painting surface, keeping the brush vertical. Pull the brush over in an arch and stop, taking the brush to a vertical position again and keeping the white on top of the stroke. For the bottom petal on the bud, with the white at the top and the brush vertical, pull the stroke down, across and up, and stop. To make petals, you will need to angle your board and angle the brush, still keeping the white to the outside edge, and pull these short, choppy strokes. Paint the buds in groups, facing different directions, and place dots in the cen-tres. Complete the buds with three fine white lines with the liner brush to represent leaves and stems. Clean brushes.

11. Little pink violets are next, made with double-loaded strokes (see page 19) and your No.3

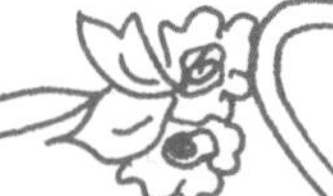

round brush. Paint them here and there, using some of the different 'pinks' on your palette. Remember that when double loading, you should reload your brush for every stroke. Position the strokes differently from the way you positioned the daisy strokes. Make two strokes at the top, then one out to each side of these. Turn your work and pull three strokes close together for the bottom wide petal. The centres consist of small dots, with a small comma stroke each side of the dots, made with the end of the stylus.

12. The trails are beginning to fill up, so now is the time to make quick little strokes, called 'fillers', to fill the gaps and tie the design together.

    Dip the end of the handle of your round or dagger brush into some pink paint, then into some white paint, put it down on the board and twirl it around. Instant roses. Place small tick leaves near these roses and along any gaps in the trails. To make tick leaves, just pick up a little paint on the tip of liner or small round brush, put the tip down gently and tick, just like with a pencil.

    Another small filler flower is a forget-me-not. Pick up some pink, white or gold on the tip of the brush and then pick up another colour. Push the paint into little five-petalled flowers. Dots complete the centres, and small tick leaves finish each flower.

13. Trace onto tracing paper the words, 'Bride's Painting Planner'. With the grey graphite paper under this tracing, trace the outline of the letters with the fine point of the stylus. Make sure that the tracing is straight, and that you have the correct side of the graphite paper under the traced letters. (Refer to Tracing the Design on page 35.) Fill in the letters with your liner brush and white paint. Allow to dry, then erase the graphite lines with your kneadable eraser.

14. Paint each corner of the clipboard with three dagger leaves, a pink and gold forget-me-not, and

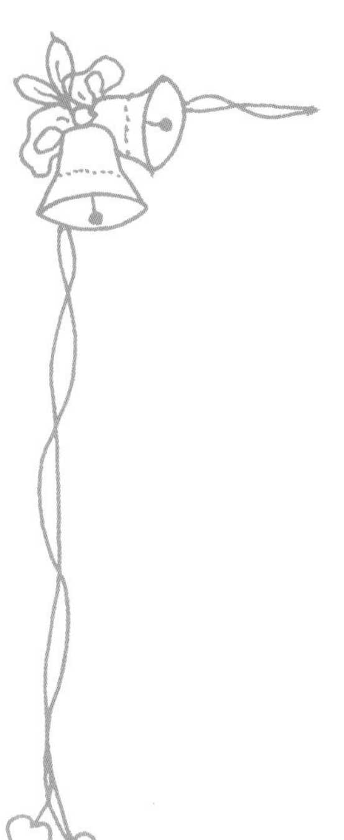

some small gold strokes with the stylus.

15. When the painting is dry, apply two coats of water-based varnish.

You have learnt so much painting this board. The only tracing was the letters, so you have done it all by yourself and made lots of painting decisions along the way. If this is the first piece you have painted, congratulations! It is a wonderful effort and I hope you enjoyed your introduction to folk painting.

Bride's

Painting Planner

Boxes and More Boxes

The traditional bride's boxes in Europe were made in wood and painted in bright colours. The designs depicted hearts, flowers, birds and often a bridal couple, complete with verses, marriage information and borders — all painted with lovely strokes and flourishes.

The boxes illustrated are for the bride or groom, or can be used to contain the rings for the wedding. I have used papier-mâché boxes, which come in all shapes and sizes and are readily available from most craft shops and department stores. The painted boxes are decorative yet very practical, and a joy to paint. They need little preparation and will last for many years. I hope you love painting them as much as I did.

BRIDE'S BEST UNDIE BOX

I found a bough of one of our gum trees broken and decided to press some of the leaves in the pages of the phone book. I had been saving a sheet of paper printed from a wildflower design by Deborah Kneen and had the idea to use this for an Australian theme. I combined the leaves and the paper to create the following design. Please use any of the lovely papers available today and omit the gum leaves if you wish. Pressed flowers also look wonderful on boxes.

TECHNIQUES
Sponging, leaf pressing, paper crafts

COLOURS
Green Oxide, Warm White, Norwegian Orange

BRUSHES
Cheap Chinese, about ½"

OTHER MATERIALS
Small ceramic sponge, sheet of 'Basket of Wild Flowers' by Deborah Kneen, scissors, craft glue,

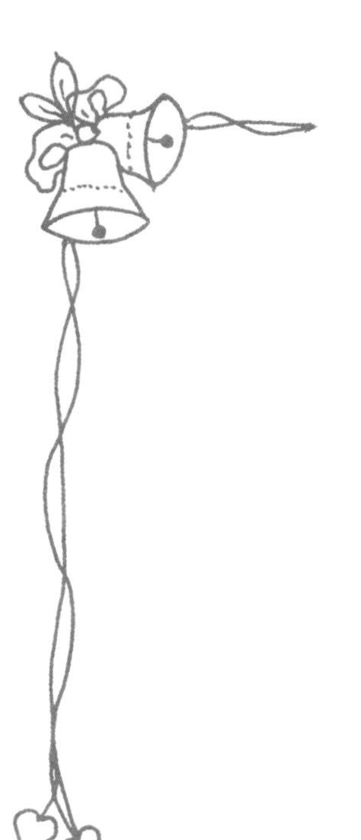

Derivan polymer gloss varnish (which binds and seals), small and large pressed or fresh gum leaves, wet and dry sandpaper, 3 m of paper tie for bow, 1 m of soft tulle, 12 small plastic rings and 2 m of narrow nylon ribbon for underwear washing bag and disposable gloves.

METHOD

1. Paint the inside of the box and lid with a mixture of Green Oxide and Warm White. Sponge the outside rim of the lid with Green Oxide and Warm White. Sponge the lid, the outside of the box and base with Norwegian Orange and Warm White. (Please refer to the colour plate.)

2. Cut out some of the baskets, individual flowers, bows and butterflies from the paper. Keep the butterflies and small flowers for the lid. Glue with Derivan other shapes inside the lid and base, for a nice surprise, and around the outside of the box. Dilute the Derivan varnish with a little water and paint over the shapes, removing all creases.

3. Glue the butterflies and small flowers on the lid.

4. Glue on the small pressed or fresh gum leaves with craft glue, fitting them around the odd shapes. Glue the larger gum leaves on the lid, allowing them to come down over the rim.

5. When the glue is dry, apply several coats of full-strength Derivan varnish, making sure that there are no gaps between the leaves and box surface. Allow to dry and sand lightly if necessary.

6. Cut several lengths of paper tie and glue them to the lid in loops. Make large bow with the paper tie and glue it onto the lid and loops. The lid looks lovely with the butterflies and small flowers tucked around the bow and leaves.

7. Varnish the inside of the box and sand well. You don't want your expensive underwear to catch.

8. To make an underwear washing and drying bag, fold the tulle in half and sew up the sides. Hem

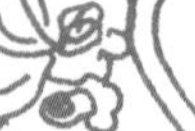

the top and sew the rings around the hem.
Thread the ribbon through.

BRIDE'S BATH BOX

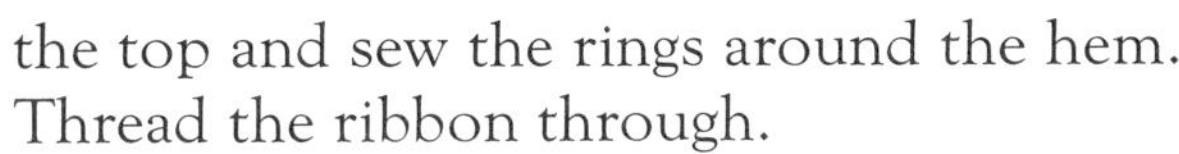

I designed this box for my daughter to use to carry
all her bath gear — she enjoys a relaxing bath. For
'the day' I embroidered a bath sheet, bought many
smelly soaps and gels, and painted the toothbrush
and soap holder to match. What a good Mother!

This box is most useful after the wedding too —
use it to store the veil, in the nursery or to store
any spare tiers of cake.

PREPARATION

While papier-mâché normally requires no pre-
painting preparation such as sealing, I thought it
should be given an extra coat of sealer. When the
painting is completed, the box can be spray
painted, making it as waterproof as possible, particularly on the base.

TECHNIQUES

Sponging, marbling, LAFS, dagger leaves, comma
strokes, stencilling, flat brush blending, dry brushing, DAS wedding shapes, liner work.

COLOURS

White basecoat, Napthol Red Light, Pale Gold,
Titanium White, Rich Gold, Colourpoint White
Pearl dimensional paint

BRUSHES

Wide basecoater, fine liner, ⅛" dagger, No.3 round,
⅛" flat

OTHER MATERIALS

Plastic wrap, feather, bow and cherub paper stencils
(from Dundas Crafts Pty Ltd, party shops and all
department stores at Christmas), Jo Sonja's Texture
Paste, Ceramacoat Sparkle Glaze (or any other
snow glaze with inbuilt sparkle), DAS and moulds,
craft glue, paper for lining inside of box (optional),
varnish.

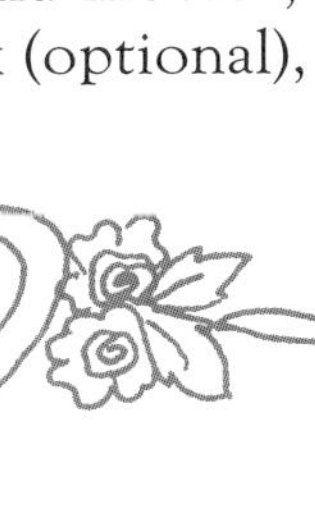

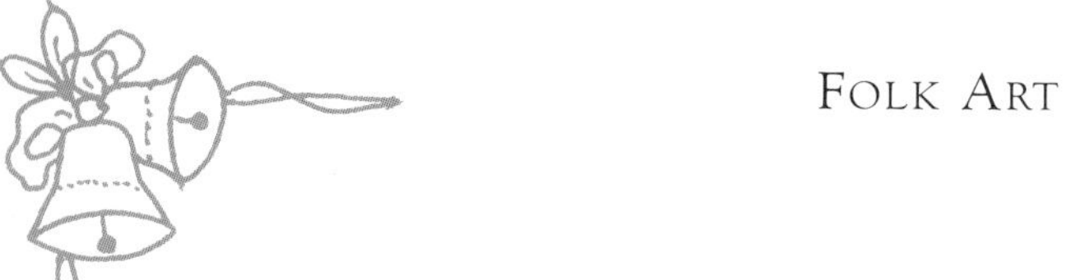
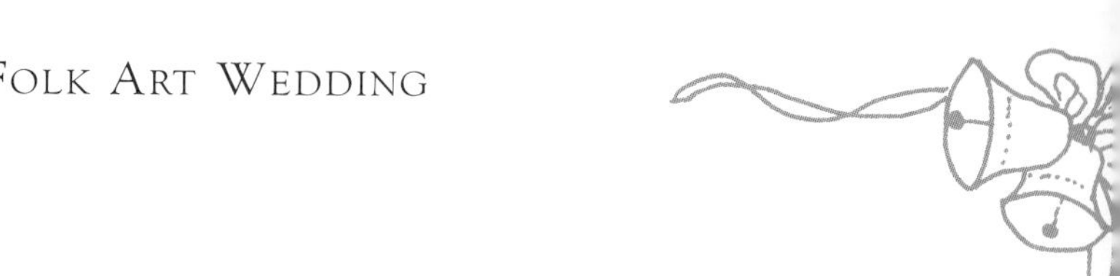

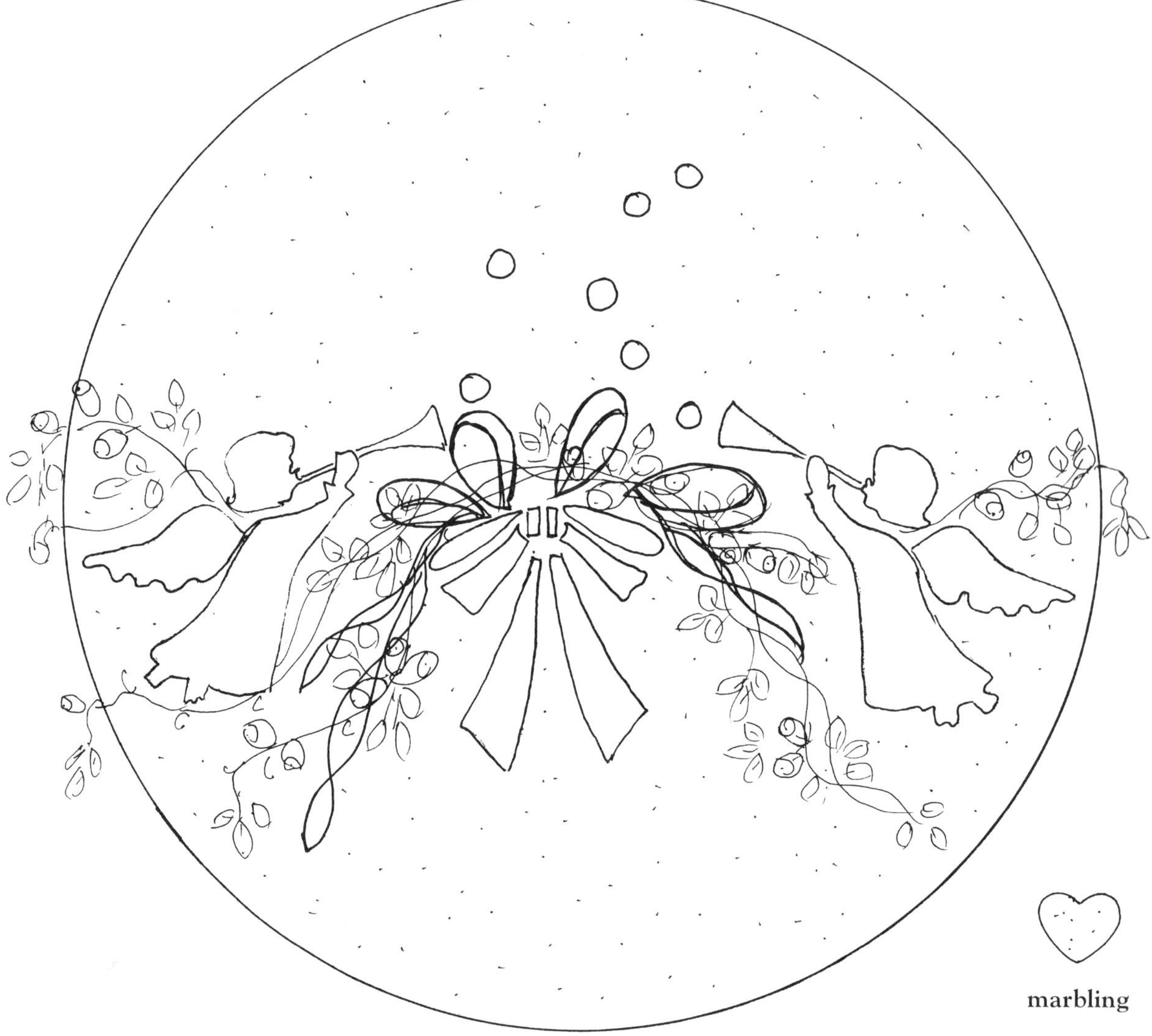

marbling

Bride's Bath Box — Lid

Method

1. Seal the box well, then basecoat white. Note that it may take several coats of white to make a good coverage.

2. Mix a fairly large quantity of White basecoat

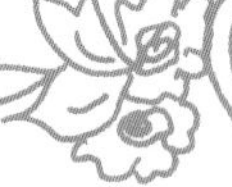

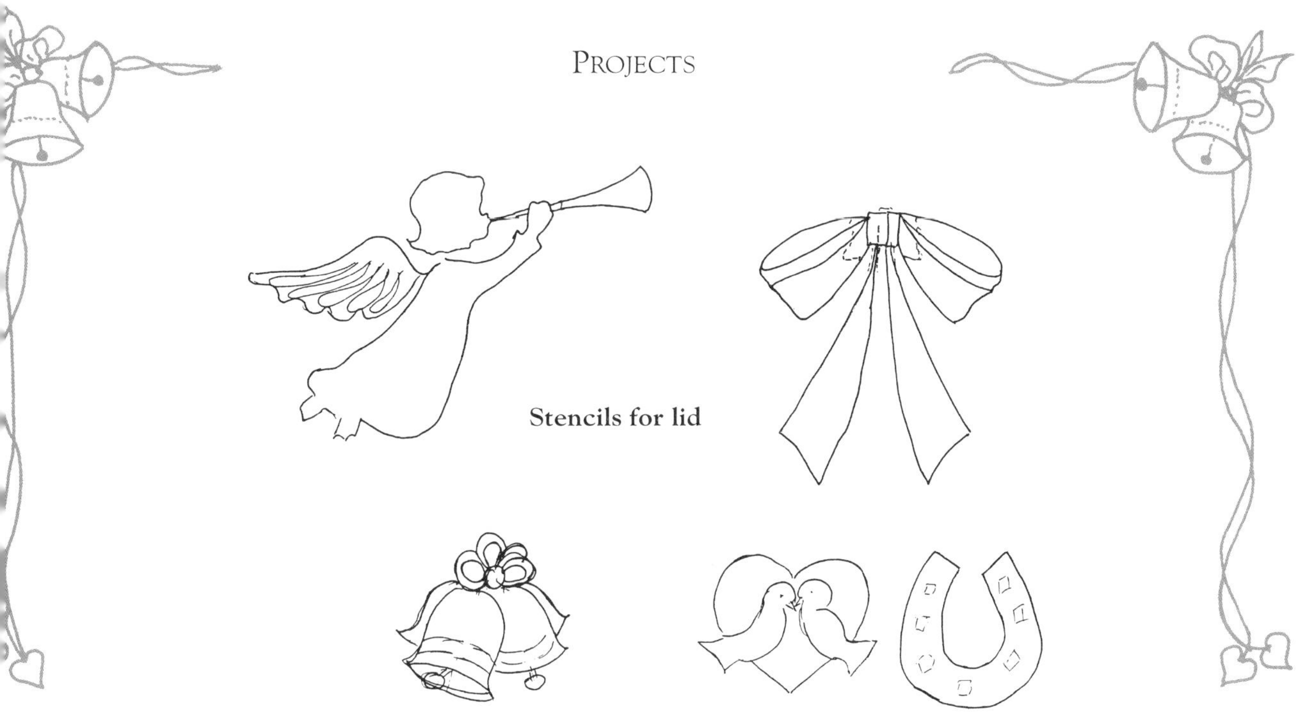

Stencils for lid

DAS shapes for sides

Bride's Bath Box

with a touch of Napthol Red Light in a small jar, making a pretty pink colour. Have your plastic wrap ready. Apply a thick coat of pink paint to the top of the lid. Immediately apply the wrap, scrunch it up and lift off. When dry, feather some fine white lines over the pink to resemble veins in rock (see Marbling on page 28.) Repeat the process on the base of the box (this is a good practice area) and around the sides of the box in an irregular line.

3. Paint the bows with Pale Gold mixed with pink and white where the DAS shapes will go. Paint in the LAFS, mixing a darker pink for some leaves and buds. White dagger leaves go on the pink and pink dagger leaves go on the white. Add small decorative commas with the Colourpoint White Pearl. Dagger Pale Gold leaves too.

4. Trace on the cherubs and bow using stencils or the design, then paint with the texture paste. The surface is meant to be rough and the wings of the cherubs grooved to resemble feathers. When dry, add glitter or the Sparkle Glaze.

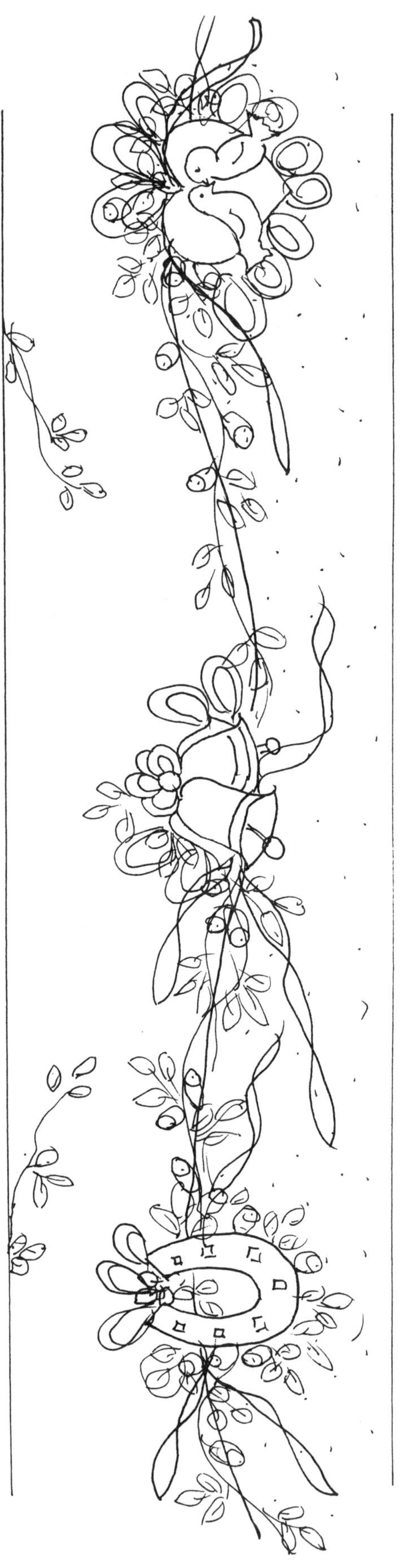

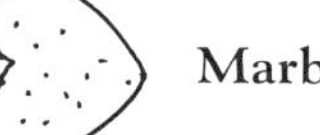

Marbling

5. The bubbles are painted with the flat brush, colour on one side of the brush and twirled around making a circle. A small dry brush of white is painted on top right and a small highlight comma stroke of Colourpoint White Pearl (please refer to Colour Plate).

6. Make the DAS wedding shapes and glue around the box. When making the DAS shapes that are to be glued around the circles, it is a good idea to bend them slightly over the circle before they are dry so that they will glue flat. See DAS Cherubs and Wedding Shapes on page 37.) Fill in with snow if there are any gaps and allow to dry. Paint more leaves and buds around these shapes.

7. With the fine liner brush, outline the bows and cherubs with a darker pink, to make them show up better. Fill in any gaps and add veins to the leaves.

8. The inside of the box and the lid can be sponged or lined with paper, then varnished to make it more waterproof.

GROOM'S GEAR BOX

We can't leave the groom out, can we? This medium-sized square box is painted with a rich red background. You will have fun filling this box with all sort of male goodies, including wedding socks and ties.

TECHNIQUES
Slip-slap background, dry brushing, round brush blending, lettering, scroll work, dots, stencilling.

COLOURS
Black basecoat, Burgundy, Napthol Red Light, Yellow Light, Rich Gold, Titanium White, Pale Gold.

BRUSHES
½" basecoater, fine liner, No.3 round.

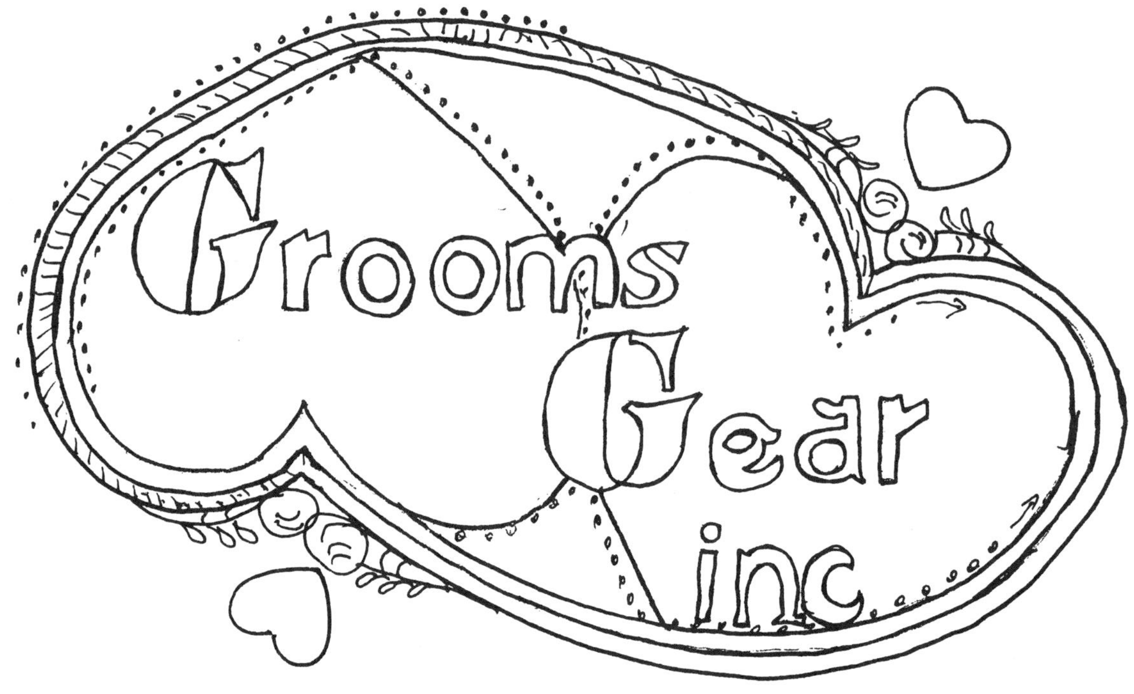

lid label

corners of lid

corners of box

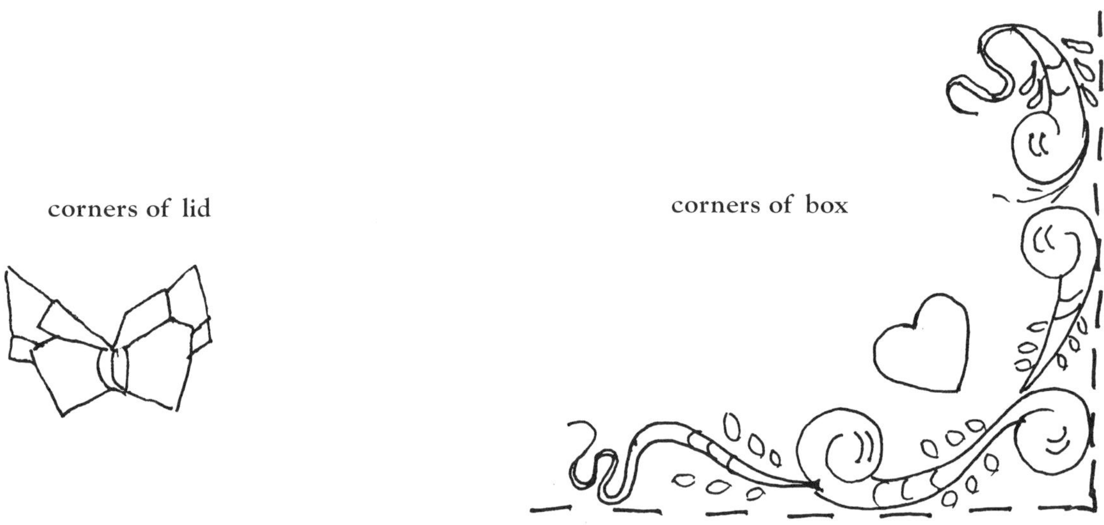

edges of lid

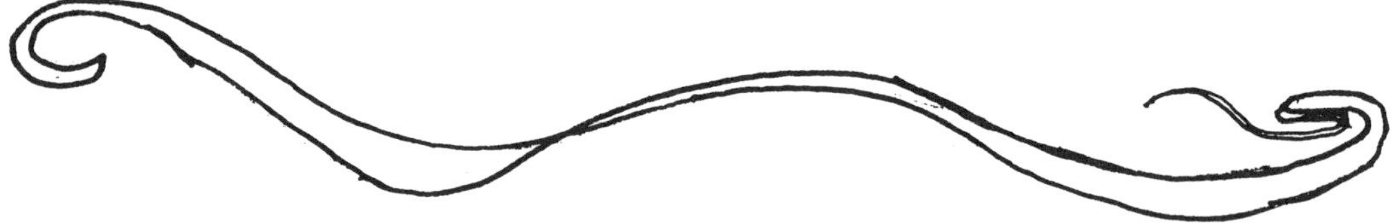

GROOM'S GEAR BOX

Other Materials

Paper towels, tracing equipment (see page 35), black waterproof pen (Artline Drawing System 0.2), Intergrain varnish, stylus or toothpick, small heart stencil, gold metallic pen (obtainable from newsagents).

Method

1. Basecoat inside the box and around the rim with Black.

2. On a palette, put out Black, Burgundy and Napthol Red Light. With the basecoater, pick up black paint and slap across and down, across and down, moving around the box. Wipe the brush on a paper towel, then pick up Burgundy and paint across and down, near the black, and over the black, across and down. Wipe the brush.

    Pick up some Napthol Red Light and repeat the process. It is this lovely colour that makes this finish — it glows like the coals in a fire.

    Paint the lid in the same way.

3. Trace the outline of the label on the lid of the box. Basecoat the hearts with two coats of Ivory. To obtain this colour, mix a tiny dash of Yellow Light into a large squeeze of Titanium White. Outline the bands around the label with two coats of Rich Gold. When dry outline with Black. When dry, outline label and hearts with Pale Gold dots made with a stylus or toothpick. Add scrolls and hearts when painting the base of box.

4. Trace the bow tie and collar in each corner of the lid and outline with the black pen. (Refer to the Colour Plate.) Paint the collar white and bow tie black, adding a little dry-brushed white to the black bow.

5. With the round brush, freehand ribbon-like lines between the corners with Rich Gold. Use thick, then thin lines. The flourishes on the ends are painted with the fine liner brush.

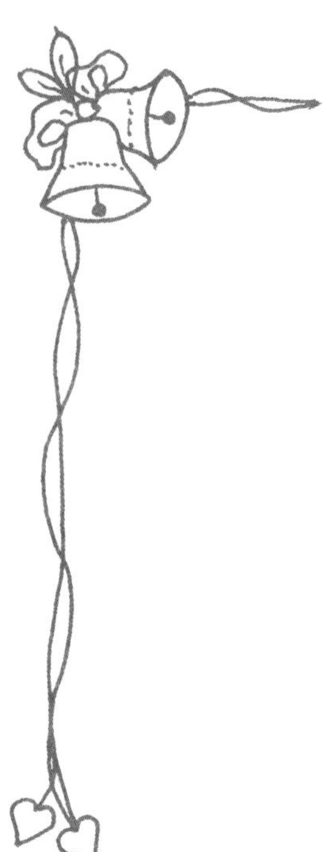

6. With the round brush, mix a tiny dash of Burgundy to some of the Ivory mix. Remove excess paint on paper towel and dry brush a little of this colour on one side of each heart to create a shadow. Wipe brush on paper towel and dry brush a little highlight with Titanium White. Allow to dry.

7. Trace the lettering. Outline with waterproof pen, then fill in with two coats of Napthol Red Light.

8. Trace, then paint the scrolls on the side corners with two coats of Rich Gold. Dry brush a little red here and there, then highlight with a dry brush of Titanium White. Decorate scrolls with fine lines of black along the scrolls, then white lines across the scrolls. With fine liner brush, paint some fine comma strokes and some flourishes.

9. Stencil or trace the hearts, then apply two coats of Rich Gold.

10. Varnish with one coat of Intergrain — Gloss for a shiny finish or Satin for a softer finish.

You can write a romantic message with the fine liner brush and Rich Gold or with the gold pen inside the lid — For His Eyes Only.

Small Ring and Gift Boxes

THE PINK HEART RING OR GIFT BOX

This charming little box could contain the gift for the flower girl, almonds for guests or earrings for the bridesmaids. It is quick and easy to paint. If you were intending to give a small gift to each guest, you could paint dozens of these boxes on a production line. A painting bee, like the quilting and patchwork bees of old, is a lot of fun and great learning and sharing experience for family and friends.

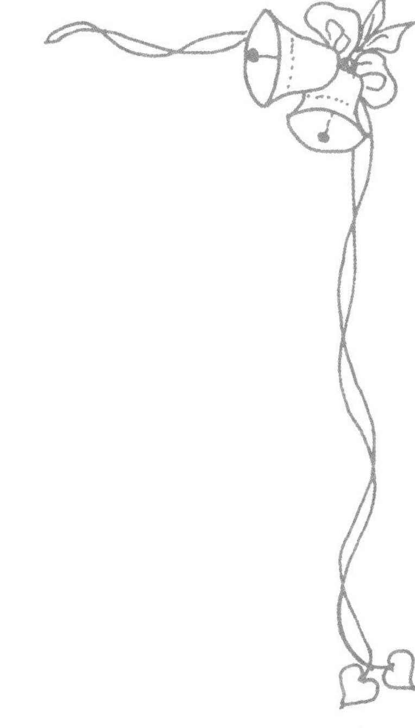

TECHNIQUES
Sponging, shading, lettering, dots, round roses, tick leaves, templates or stencilling.

COLOURS
Plum Pink or Green Oxide basecoat, Warm White, Rich or Pale Gold, Plum Pink, Green Oxide.

BRUSHES
Basecoater, fine liner, No.3 round.

OTHER MATERIALS
Tracing equipment (see page 35), pencil, stylus or toothpick, small sea or ceramic sponge, Helix H23 initial stencil from stationers and newsagents, water-based varnish.

METHOD
1. Basecoat the inside of the box. If painting a number of boxes, then a Plaid FolkArt basecoat would be more economical.

2. Trace Heart onto the lid. Pencil an uneven line around the bottom of the box. Basecoat inside heart and bottom of base with two coats of Warm White. When dry sponge over this with a mixture of Warm White and Rich or Pale Gold.

3. Basecoat the rest of the box with one coat of Plum Pink. When dry, sponge with a Plum Pink, Warm White and Rich or Pale Gold.

4. With round brush dab a line of Plum Pink on the pink side of the demarcation line and Pale or Rich Gold on the white side of the line.

5. Trace and transfer the initial to the heart, or use the initial stencil. With liner brush paint the initial with two coats of Plum Pink. If desired, thin a little Plum Pink with water, and paint in the shaded area. Lightly dry brush Warm White for a highlight at the top of the initial. (refer to the design and Colour Plate.)

6. Finish the box with gold dots, green tick leaves and round roses. Apply gold dots with the stylus

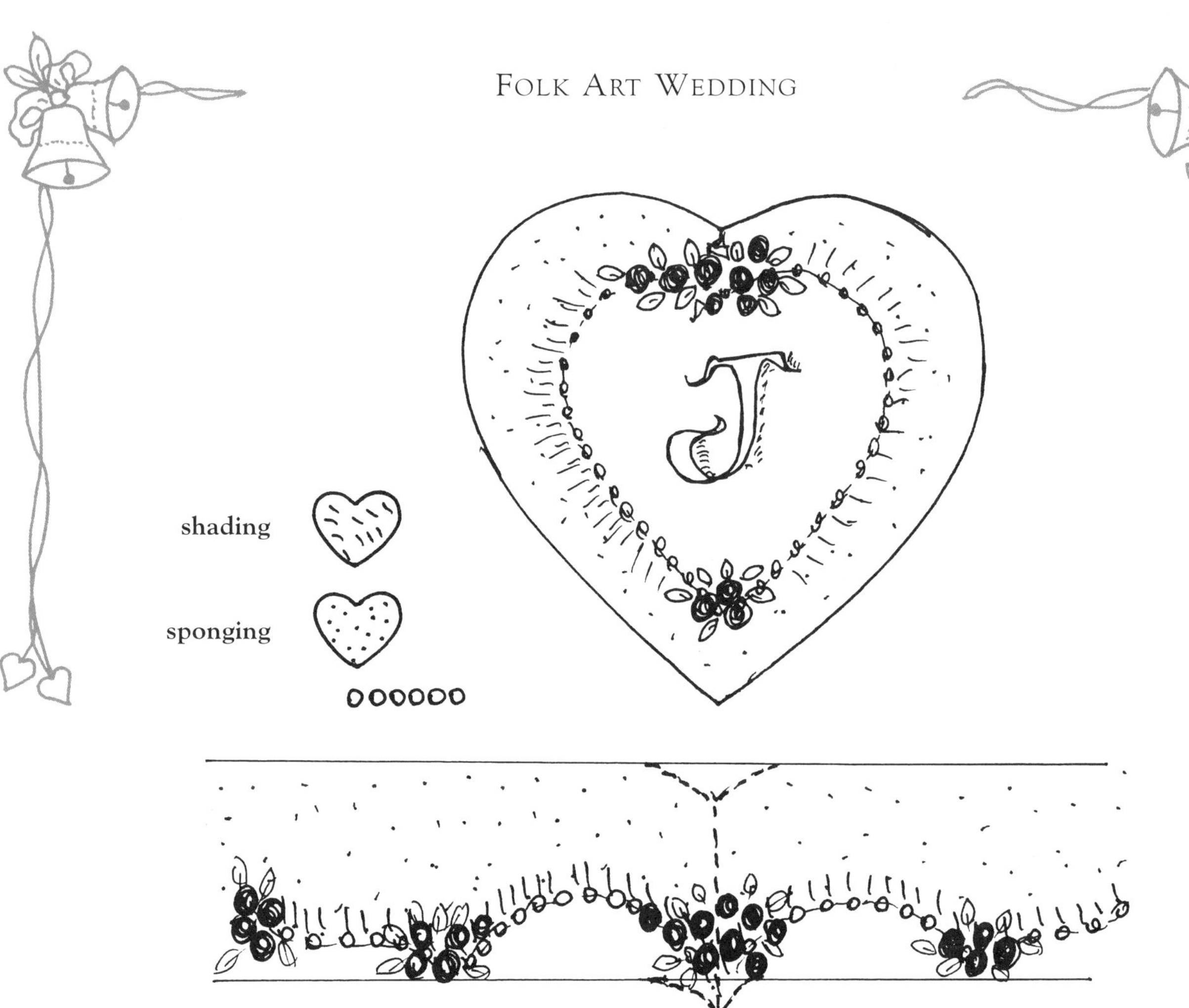

shading

sponging

PINK HEART RING OR GIFT BOX

or toothpick along the outline. For the roses, put out a small dab of Plum Pink and Warm White and using the end of the handle of the liner brush, pick up one and then the other colour. Apply and turn the handle to create a swirl, each resembling a tiny rose. Place in groups along the borders and top and bottom of the heart. For tick leaves, with a liner brush pick up a small amount of Green Oxide and position little tick leaves around the roses. (Refer to colour plate.)

7. Varnish when dry.

HEARTS AND DOVE RING BOX

This small heart box is also an ideal shape for a ring box. Allow plenty of time for this box, as the dimensional paint takes approximately 72 hours to dry and cure.

HEARTS AND DOVES RING BOX

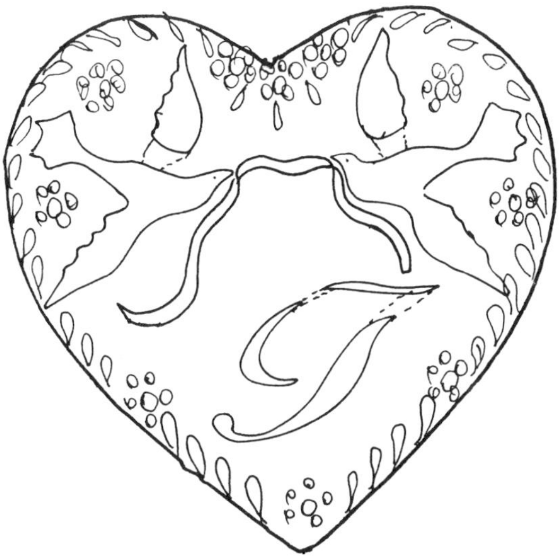

stencils and design on lid

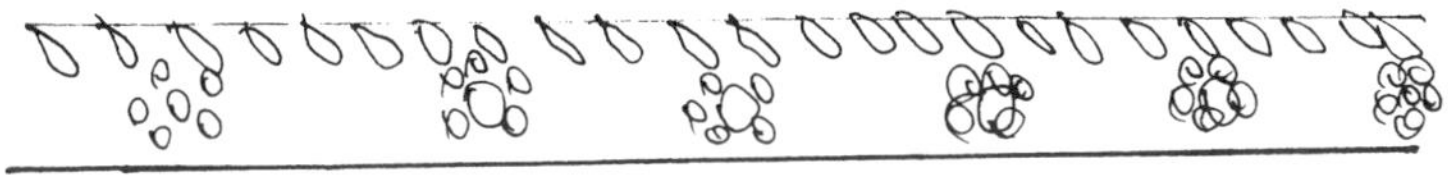

rim of lid

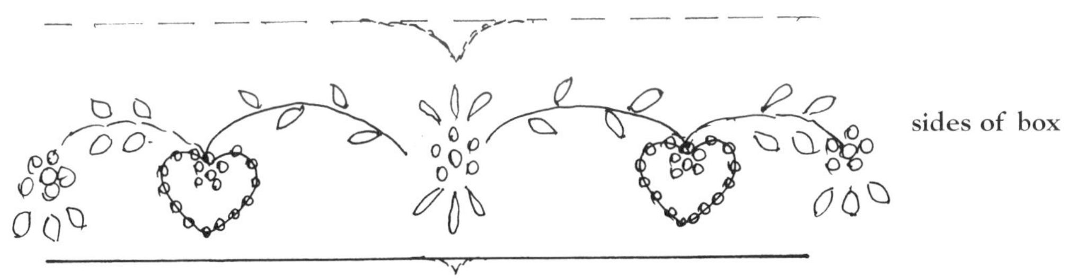

sides of box

TECHNIQUES

Stencilling, liner work, dots, comma strokes, lettering, dry brushing.

COLOURS

Titanium White, Pale Gold, Rich Gold, Colourpoint Pearl dimensional paint, Ultramarine Blue.

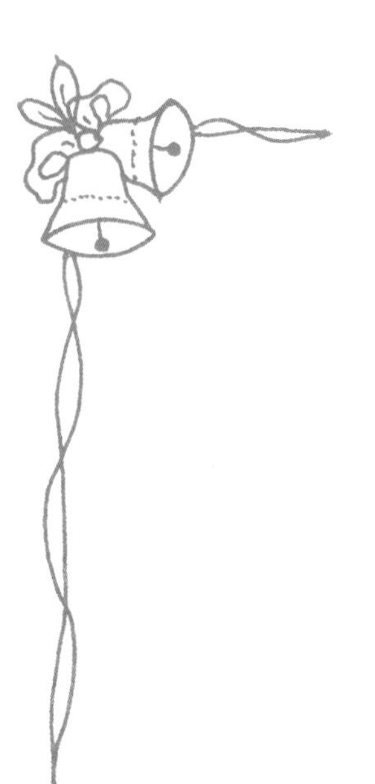

BRUSHES

Basecoater, No.3 round, fine liner.

OTHER MATERIALS

Plaid Monogram stencil has doves, hearts and initials (from craft shops). Letter stencils also available from newsagents. Pencil, Jo Sonja's Texture Paste, water-based varnish.

METHOD

1. Basecoat inside and outside of the box with three coats of Titanium White. A good coverage is needed.

2. Stencil the hearts around the outside of the box with two coats of Pale Gold. (Refer to the colour plate for placement.) Allow to dry. Then dry brush a little Rich Gold on one side of each heart and a little Titanium White on the other side for a highlight. Using the liner brush and Rich Gold, connect the hearts with a fine line.

3. Using the Colourpoint Pearl, make fine strokes along the lines connecting the hearts, and at the top of the hearts. Make the flowers between the hearts with dots. Paint a border of comma strokes on the lid. When dry, paint the comma strokes Rich Gold.

4. Trace the doves and initial stencils. Using the round brush, paint the doves with Texture Paste, building it up until you have fat doves. If desired, paint over with a little Colourpoint Pearl to add a lustre. With Colourpoint Pearl draw a line resembling a ribbon held by the doves. When dry, paint with Rich Gold. The initial can be painted and built up with Colourpoint Pearl or Texture Paste if you wish to achieve a more dimensional look. When dry, paint over the Rich or Pale Gold.

5. This is a very delicate-looking box and you may not want to add to it, but I dry brushed a little Ultramarine Blue on the flowers and on some of the strokes. Give the flowers gold centres.

ANTIQUED GOLD-LEAFED CHERUB GIFT BOX

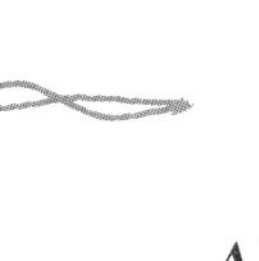

You might decide that earrings are your gift to the bridesmaids, in which case this would make the perfect presentation box.

TECHNIQUES
Marbling, DAS cherub, gold leafing, antiquing, dagger leaves, liner work, dots.

COLOURS
Green Oxide, Pthalo Green, Brilliant Green, Rich Gold, Pale Gold.

BRUSHES
Basecoater, No 3 round, ⅛" dagger, fine liner

OTHER MATERIALS
Paper towels, tracing equipment (see page 35), Kleister medium, plastic wrap, DAS and cherub mould, gold leafing materials (see page 30), antiquing materials (see page 39), craft glue, water-based varnish.

METHOD

1. Basecoat the whole box with a mix of Green Oxide and Pthalo Green. At least two coats are needed.

2. Paint the rim of the lid with two coats of Brilliant Green.

3. Mix Rich Gold with the Kleister medium and marble with plastic wrap over the entire box. (Refer to Marbling on page 28.)

4. Make a DAS cherub. (Refer to DAS Cherubs and Wedding Shapes on page 37.) When the cherub is dry, Gold Leaf or paint with two coats of Rich Gold. (Refer Gold Leafing on page 30.) Apply one coat water-based varnish. Brush with antiquing mix, and wipe off until you like the effect. (Refer to Antiquing on page 39.)

5. Make a mark where the cherub will be glued.

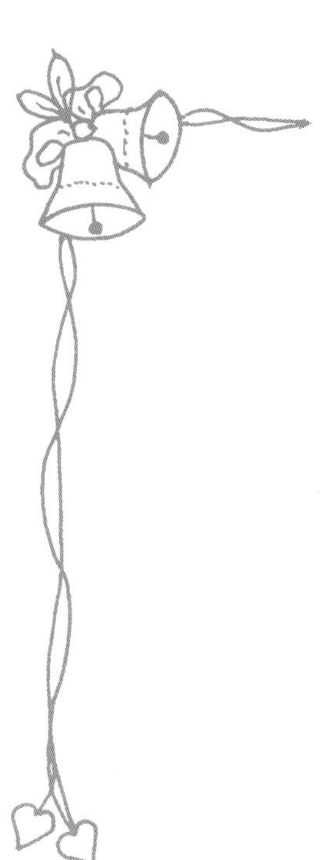

With the dagger brush, paint groups of three leaves using different greens around the spot where the cherub will go. Make veins and stems with the liner brush and Pale Gold. Add gold dots around the border and near the leaves.

6. Glue on the cherub. Apply one coat of water-based varnish on cherub and box.

Half Pots and Pots

Pots in all shapes and sizes are available in terracotta, which is an orange colour, and bisque, which can be white or a biscuit colour. Both provide good painting surfaces and need only a wash in water before painting. The half pots can be obtained from craft, garden and hobby ceramic shops.

You could fill your painted pots with flowers, balloons and candles, and tie them with large bows and tulle. Small cherubs glued on would also look lovely.

There are lots of places for these pots — tied onto church doors, tied onto the flower girl's arm, on the cake or on the tables, or scattered around the reception room. They would enhance the garden for an outdoor wedding. Just let your imagination soar.

I backed the half pots with cardboard before painting them, filled them with small rosebuds, glued them onto ribbon and tulle, then used narrow ribbon to tie them onto the pews in the church.

A glue gun is a bride's best friend when making lots of pew decorations. The tie-on ribbons for pew decorations can be glued on last at the back of the completed decorations. All ribbons are suitable, including the narrow gift type.

Note that it you want to fill the pots with fresh flowers, you will need to insert a container to hold the water.

WHITE BISQUE HALF POTS FOR PEWS

TECHNIQUES
LAFS, liner work, filler flowers, tick leaves

COLOURS
Napthol Red Light, Warm White, Green Oxide

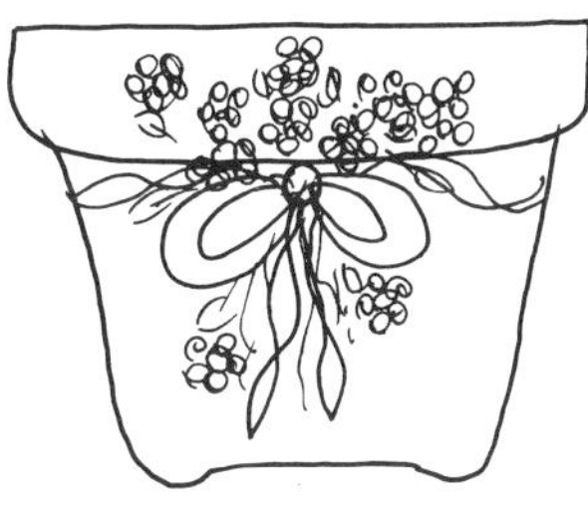

WHITE BISQUE HALF POT

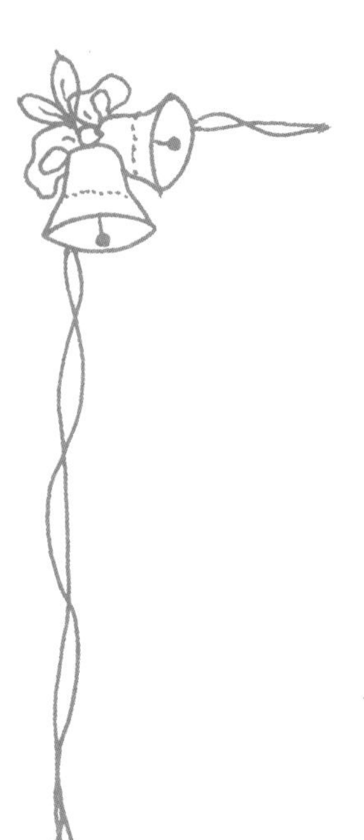

Brushes
No 3 round, ⅛" dagger, fine liner

Other Materials
Pencil, scissors, white cardboard, clear craft glue or glue gun, wide and narrow ribbon, tulle, fresh pink rosebuds.

Method
1. Mix Napthol Red Light and Warm White to make a pale pink and paint a small bow.
2. Paint the stems with the fine liner and Green Oxide.
3. Pick up the pink mix and Warm White and make some small buds and filler flowers. Paint some tiny tick leaves in Green Oxide around the flowers.
4. Cut out the white cardboard backing and glue onto the pots. Glue the ribbons and large tulle bows onto the cardboard. Allow narrow ribbon for tying onto the pews. Fill pots with small bunches of pink silk rosebuds.

GREEN HALF POTS FOR PEWS

Techniques
Sponging, dots, cross-hatching, LAFS

Colours
Pthalo Green, Green Oxide, Titanium White, Norwegian Orange, Warm White

Brushes
Basecoater, scungy, fine liner, No.3 round

Other Materials
Paper towels, clear craft glue or glue gun, white cardboard, ribbons, tulle.

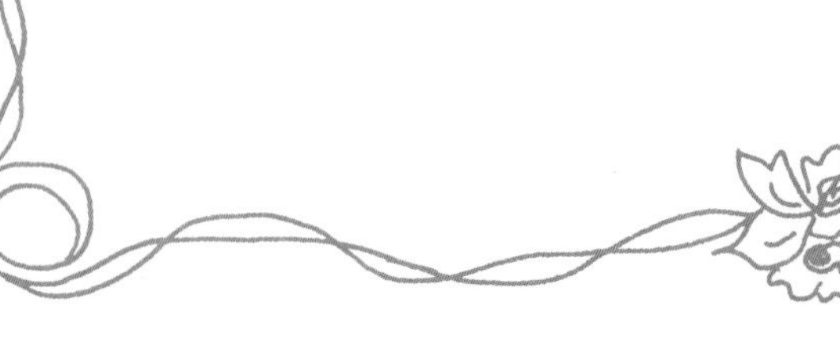

Method

Sponged pots

1. Basecoat with a mix of Pthalo Green and Green Oxide.
2. Lightly sponge the rim of the pot with scungy brush and greens and Titanium White. Apply small strokes and dots in white. (Refer to the colour plate.)

Wisteria pots

1. Basecoat the pot with the green mix. Paint the rim with the green mix plus a little Norwegian Orange.
2. Cross-hatch in white with the liner brush. To cross-hatch, paint thin lines diagonally across the pot in one direction, then paint lines going in the opposite direction to create diamond shapes.
3. A peachy colour is made by mixing a little Norwegian Orange with Warm White. Using the point of the round brush, stipple or pounce filler flowers with this peach mix.
4. Back the pots with cardboard, decorate with ribbons and tulle and tie to the pews.

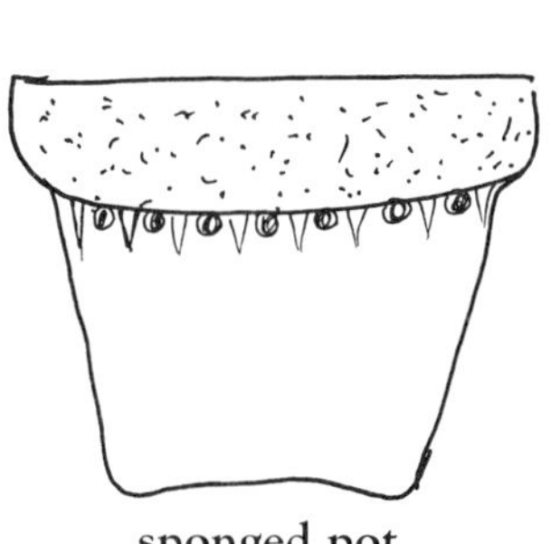

sponged pot

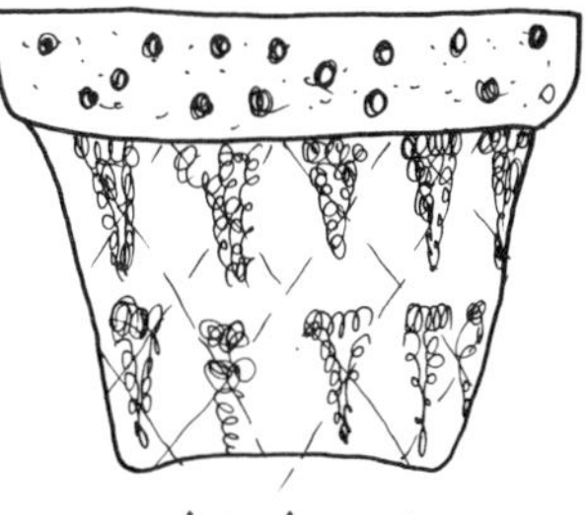

wisteria pot

Green Half Pots

PEACH AND GOLD CHERUB POTS

These pots are designed to decorate the tables.

Techniques
DAS cherub, sponging, tick leaves, filler flowers

Colours
Norwegian Orange, Warm White, Rich Gold, Green Oxide

Brushes
Basecoater, No.3 round, fine liner

Other Materials
DAS and cherub mould, ceramic or sea sponge, paper towels, clear craft glue or glue gun, white cardboard, ribbon, flowers or greenery or candles

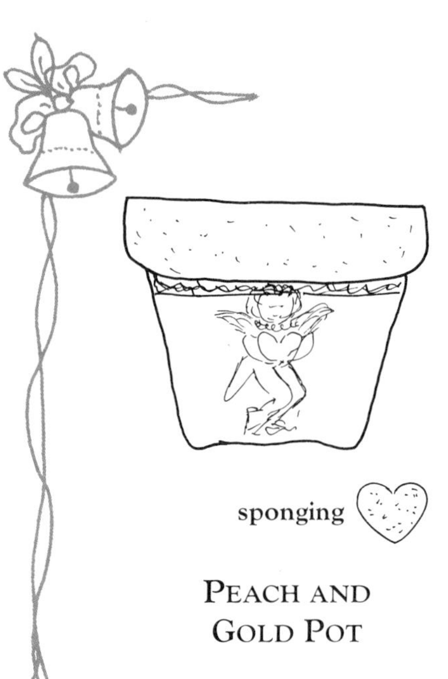

sponging

Peach and Gold Pot

Method

1. Make the DAS Cherub. (Refer to DAS Cherubs and Wedding Shapes on page 37.)
2. Make up a peach mix with a little Norwegian Orange and Warm White. Basecoat the pot with this mix. Lightly sponge Rich Gold and Peach onto the rim of the pot.
3. Paint a Rich Gold band about 1 cm (⅜") wide under the rim.
4. Pale the peach colour with Warm White and lightly paint the cherub. Lightly shade around the legs and arms with peach if desired.
5. Paint the heart and quiver with Rich Gold.
6. With the tip of the liner brush, dab some little green tick leaves and filler flowers under the cherub's neck.
7. Glue loops of ribbon inside the pots and fill them with flowers and greenery, or long candles.

BLUE LAPIS LAZULI POT

This finish would also be suitable for a small ring box, but I decided to paint a larger pot for you to practise on.

Technique

Faux Lapis Lazuli

Colours

Ultramarine Blue, Black, Burgundy, Aqua, Yellow Oxide, Rich Gold, Warm White

Brushes

Basecoater, old scungy or cheap Chinese (large for large pot, small for small pot), fine liner

Other Materials

Water-based varnish, plastic tray, paper towels, old toothbrush, wet and dry sandpaper, clear craft glue or glue gun, DAS and cherub mould, if desired, chocolates or flowers

METHOD

1. Basecoat the pot with two coats of Ultramarine Blue. When dry, apply one coat of varnish.

2. On a plastic tray put out a small amount of each colour. With a scungy brush, lightly sponge on colours in the following order. You are aiming to create drifts of colour around the pot. If you are working on a larger item, it pays to do a little at a time. Just dab lightly — you want a furry effect, no blobs. Wipe the brush on a paper towel between colour changes, but do not wash it.

COLOUR 1

Dab a little Black here and there in drifts

COLOUR 2

Mix a little Burgundy and Ultramarine Blue to make purple and drift here and there.

COLOUR 3

Drift Aqua. Don't overdo it — you can always repeat the process.

COLOUR 4

Drift Yellow Oxide sparingly here and there.

COLOUR 5

Mix the Yellow Oxide and Ultramarine Blue to make a little green and drift here and there.

3. At this stage examine the effect. Drift in a little more Ultramarine Blue, then Black, and tie all the colours together. Repeat any colours if you have overdone these filler colours.

4. Using a fine liner brush and Rich Gold, wiggle some very fine vein lines and small specks near the Yellow Oxide drifts.

5. Apply one coat of varnish.

6. Mix some Warm White with water, and very lightly spatter, using the old toothbrush. You are after a very fine mist here and there.

7. Dry well, then apply another coat of varnish. If you would like a highly polished finish, you will need to apply many coats of varnish, giving a light fine sand every now and again.

8. Decorate the pot and glue on a DAS cherub if desired. Fill with chocolates, candles or flowers.

Cherubs and Angels

Cherubs are depicted as sweet, soft, smiling, impish and childlike, winging their way around the world holding bows and arrows and garlands of flowers. They are second in pecking order to the angels, the spiritual beings who serve God. Many people sincerely believe in angels and see them in human form with wings. Most see them as females.

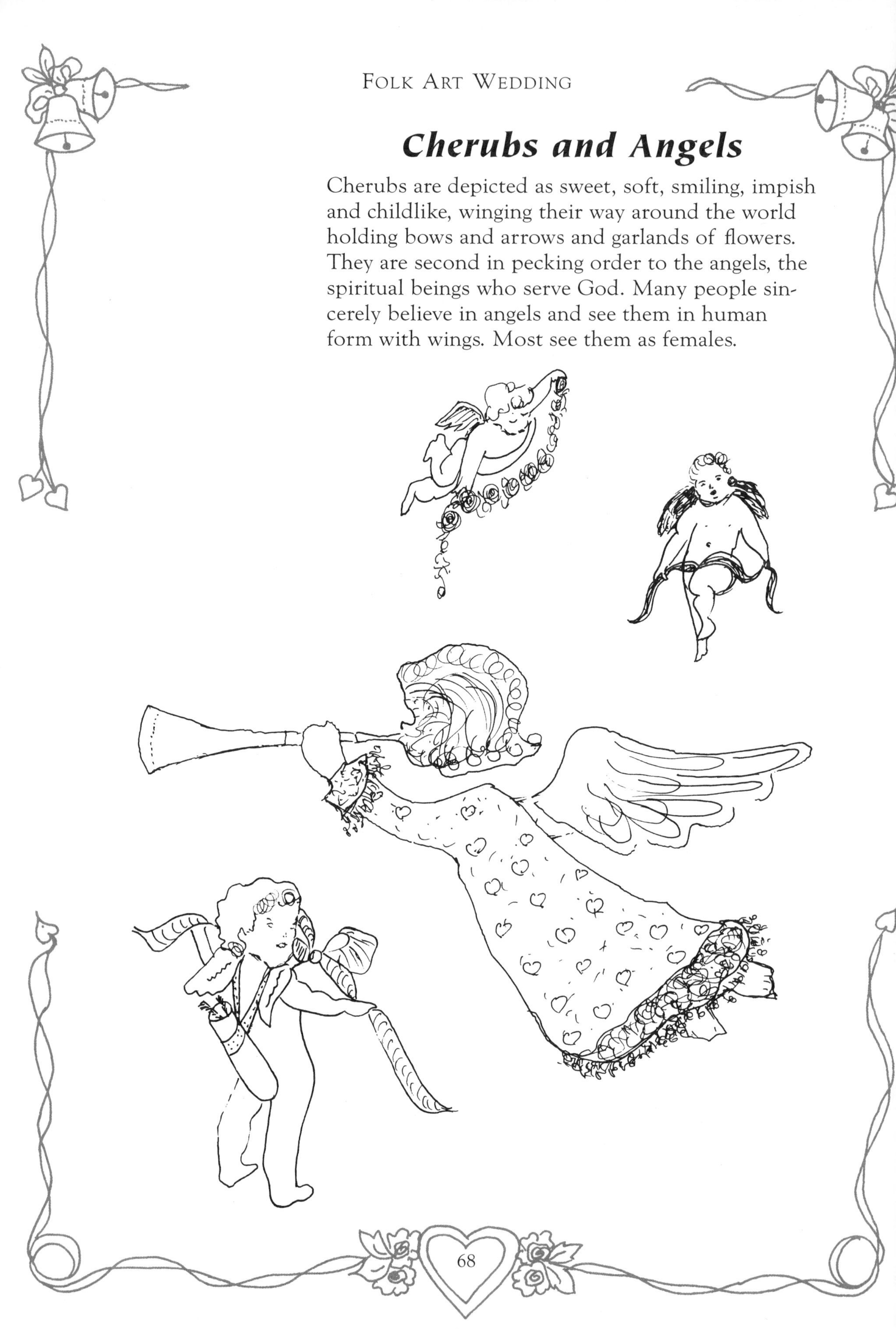

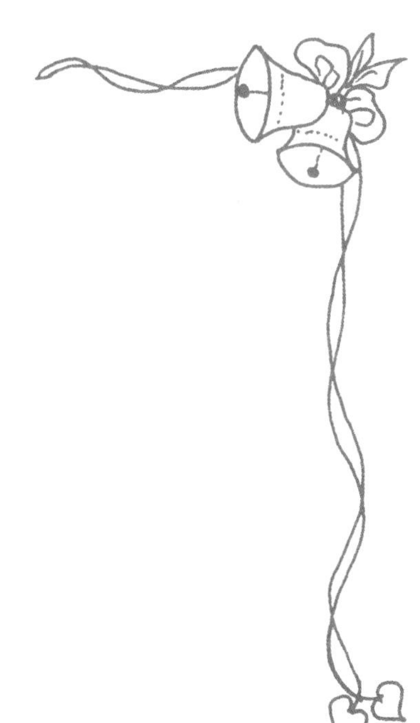

Whether one believes in angels or not, brides are high on their visiting list.

Cherubs and angels are found in craft shops, garden shops and supermarkets, especially at Christmas. They are inexpensive, being made from clay, paper or plastic. They do not mind being painted, or made into chocolate and paper shapes.

My daughter said to me that she wanted a 'lovey, dovey, romantic wedding'. She had white tulle, red roses, orange blossom, pearls, candles and a string quartet, but it was the cherubs and angels scattered here and there at her wedding, and now in this book, that added romance, nostalgia and the extra dimension

PAINTED CHOCOLATE BOWLS

These small woven wood bowls were found in the supermarket at a very reasonable price. They seemed to be the ideal containers for the chocolates that were to be served with the coffee at the reception. The cherubs were made for the bridal table, while the wedding mould was used for the guests. The ceramic cherubs were bought at a ceramic shop. They had been cleaned and fired and needed only painting. You may be able to find a similar cherub in plastic or papier-mâché in cake-decorating shops. Florists are another source of supply.

TECHNIQUES
LAFS, flat brush blending

COLOURS
Delphinium Blue basecoat, Blue Sapphire metallic (FolkArt brand), Warm White, Rich Gold

BRUSHES
Basecoater, ⅛" dagger, ⅛" flat fine liner

OTHER MATERIALS
Wet and dry sandpaper or sealer (such as Jo Sonja's All Purpose Sealer), paper towels, ceramic or plastic cherubs, craft glue

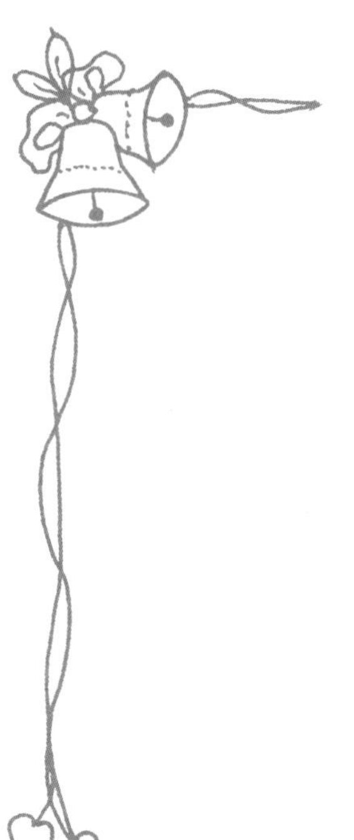

Method

1. Lightly sand the bowls before painting, or seal them. The surface may need to be roughened a little so that the paint or sealer will grab. Apply two coats of the basecoat to the bowls. (Because you will be painting a number of these bowls, it is more economical to buy the larger containers of basecoat.) Then apply a coat of Blue Sapphire metallic over the top.

2. Paint some small trails with the liner brush and some small leaves with the dagger brush. (Refer to Light Airy Fairy Style on page 25.) Small buds and roses also look pretty. (Refer to Flat Brush Blending on page 21.)

3. Apply two coats of Rich Gold to the cherubs and glue one on each bowl.

RAINBOW RICE OR ROSE PETAL BOWL

Confetti is rarely permitted these days, but alternatives include rose petals, potpourri and rice.

Traditionally, the flower girls preceded the bride, throwing rose petals down the aisle to the altar. Today guests bring their own petals or rice, or a container is provided for them. This painted bowl is placed in the vestibule or outside the church. After the wedding ceremony, when the happy couple is outside, a designated person offers the bowl to the guests. They immediately scatter the contents over the lucky recipients, who squeal with delight, especially when it is forced down their necks!

For a large wedding it may be necessary to paint two containers. They are quite useful afterwards for fruit. Once again, I used woven wood bowls from the supermarket, as they are the most inexpensive.

Techniques

Sponging, washed, round brush blending, dry brushing, dots, line work.

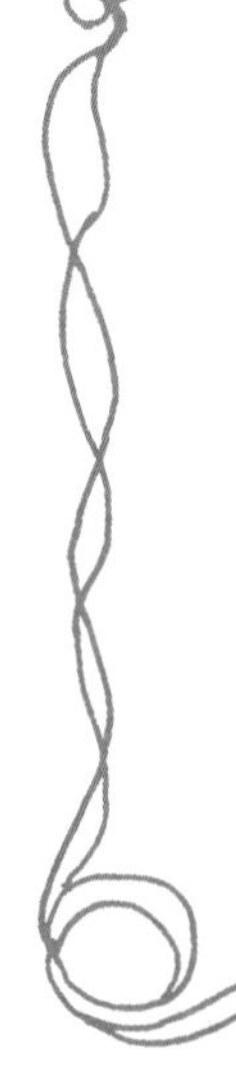

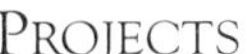

Colours

Rainbow colours (pink, green, blue, mauve, yellow)
for sponging, Pale Gold metallic, Silver metallic,
White Pearl metallic, Rich Gold metallic, Plum
Pink, Green Oxide, Burgundy, Titanium White.

Brushes

No.3 round, fine liner

Other Materials

Wet and dry sandpaper, sealer (such as Jo Sonja's
All Purpose Sealer), ceramic or sea sponge, tracing
supplies (see page 35, and use blue graphite paper),
plastic cherub, craft glue, ribbon

Method

1. Sand and seal the bowl.

2. Sponge the rainbow colours in drifts across the
   bowl. Sponge the outside first to see the effect.
   Allow to dry, then sponge inside. At first the
   colours look very bright, but the washes will
   tone them down.

3. Mix up thin washes of the metallic paints. First,
   paint each side with a Pale Gold wash. Allow to
   dry, then follow with a Silver wash, a White
   Pearl wash and a Rich Gold wash, drying
   between washes. You should end up with a glow-
   ing effect. Mine looked a little like lustre glass.
   (Refer to the colour plate.)

4. Trace on the heart flowers design.

5. Basecoat the flower petals Plum Pink and the
   leaves Green Oxide. Refer to Round Brush
   Blending on page 20 and Dry Brushing on page
   26. Put out a small amount of Burgundy and
   with the round brush blend over the Plum Pink
   some shading from the centre. Note that two
   petals on the side of each flower are darker. For
   the paler petals and buds pull out some fine
   Burgundy lines with the liner brush. Paint the
   centres Burgundy. Put out some Titanium White
   into the Burgundy. It should look like light and

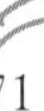

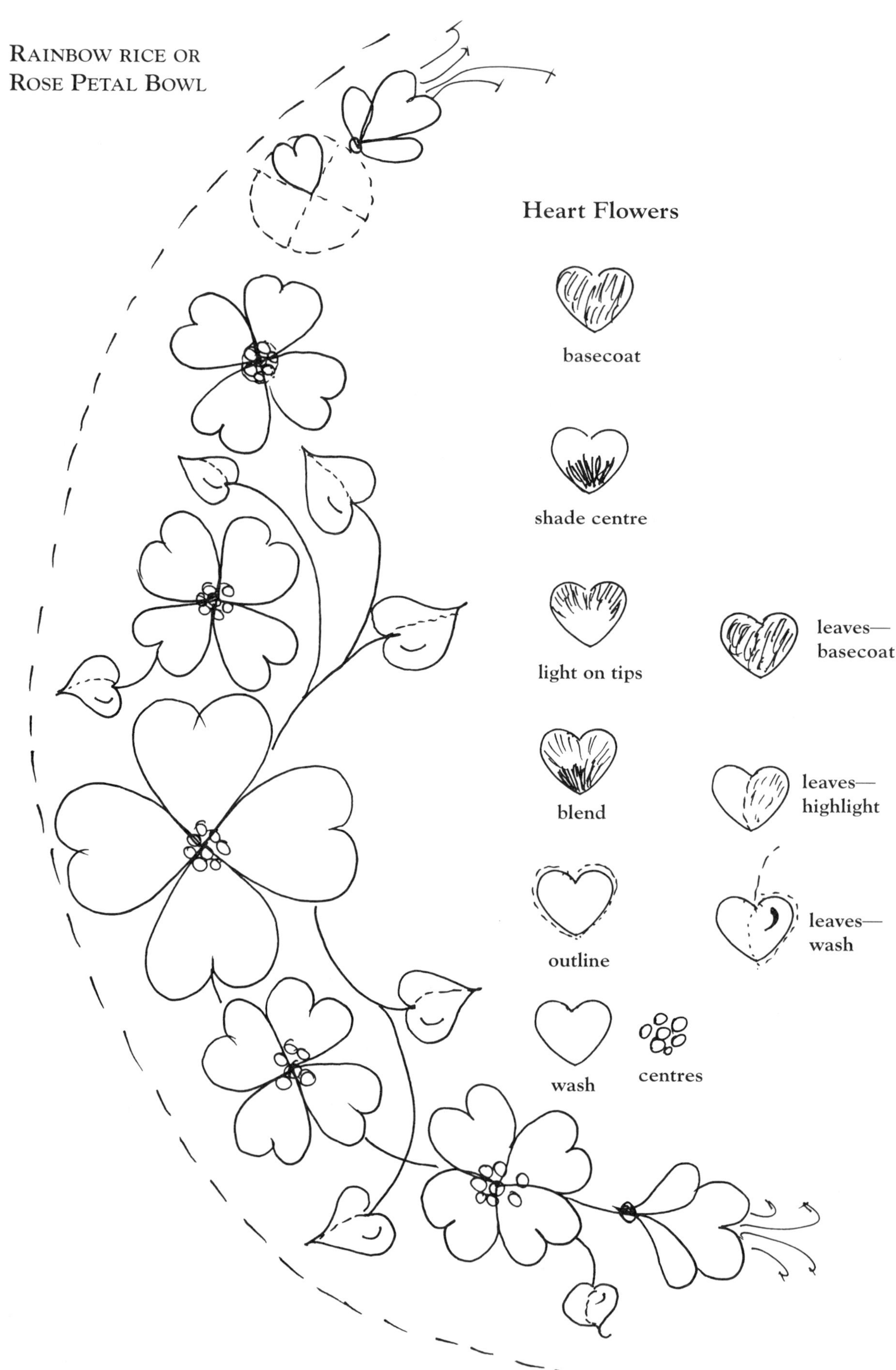

RAINBOW RICE OR
ROSE PETAL BOWL

Heart Flowers

basecoat

shade centre

light on tips

blend

outline

wash

centres

leaves—
basecoat

leaves—
highlight

leaves—
wash

shade, yet subtly blended. Two petals and the buds should have more Titanium White than Burgundy. Refer to Colour Plate. The centres are a circle of Titanium White dots with a larger dot in the middle. A single dot is at the base of each bud. When dry, the petals are dry brushed with Pearl White to tone down the colours and blend into the bowl colours.

6. Dry brush the leaves on one side only with Titanium White. Make a small white comma stroke with the stylus for highlight.

7. Paint the stems in Green Oxide, then outline the whole design in Titanium White with a fine liner brush.

8. Basecoat the cherub Silver, then wash over it Pale Gold, Plum Pink. White Pearl and Silver until you like the result. Glue onto bowl.

9. Glue large bow of pretty ribbon onto the back of the bowl. Ribbons today are quite glorious — they are made from many lustrous fibres and printed in many patterns. Fill the bowl with rose petals, rice or potpourri. If you would like coloured rice to match your colour scheme, then rice dyeing is for you. Just add a few drops of food colouring to uncooked rice — a little goes a long way. Mix different coloured rice for rainbow rice. Dry on a tray. The birds are going to love this.

SIMPLY STRIPED CANDLES

I found these candles, complete with cherubs at a discount shop — the candles were white and the cherubs were gold. The secret is to seal where the paint will go, but leave the top unpainted. Only use water-based sealers such as Jo Sonja's Sealer.

TECHNIQUE
Dripping diluted paint

COLOURS
Dark Pink, Medium Pink, Light Pink, Warm

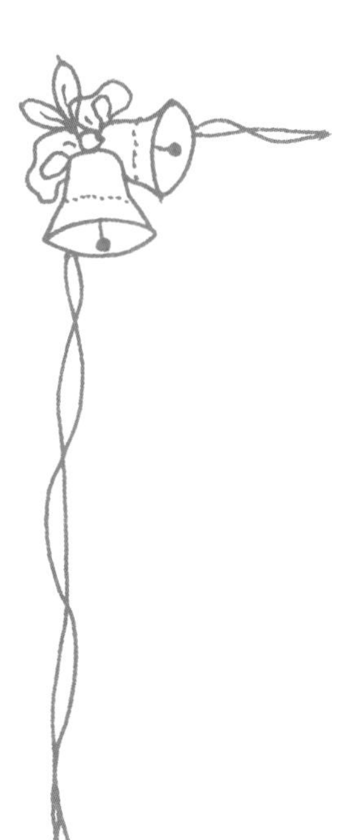

White, Silver, White Pearl, Rich Gold

Brushes
Nos 3 and 8 round

Other Materials
Sealer, such as Jo Sonja's All Purpose Sealer, paper towels, hair dryer

Method

1. Paint each candle with three coats of sealer. Basecoat with Dark Pink, leaving the cherub gold if desired.

2. Mix the different colours with water. Alternate the small and larger round brush to control the size of the drips. Fill the brush with one colour and press against the top of the candle here and there. The paint runs down the candle, forming little channels that resemble melted wax. Dry using the hair dryer, then repeat the dribbling process with the other colours. Dry between each coat. Apply full strength paint for final dribbles.

3. The angelic violinist on this candle was given many washes, finishing with Dark Pink and Rich Gold.

GOLD LEAF CANDLEHOLDER

Candleholders come in many shapes and sizes, from standing models to wall sconces. The one illustrated is made from wood and was bought at a large department store. It is suitable for the bridal table, the church and later at home. It can be painted in your choice of colours. A matching pair of candleholders would look lovely on the dining-room table.

I found the angel in a supermarket. It was made of plastic and was found amongst Christmas decorations.

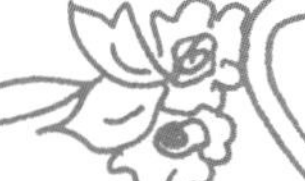

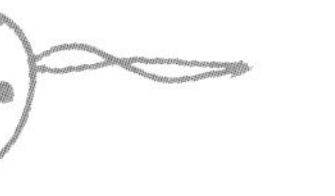

TECHNIQUES
Marbling, gold leafing, spattering

COLOURS
Pthalo Green, Green Oxide, Rich Gold, Jade Green, Yellow Oxide

BRUSHES
Basecoater, large round, old toothbrush

OTHER MATERIALS
Masking tape, water-based varnish, crumpled foil or plastic, plastic wrap, gold leafing materials (see page 30 — you will need several sheets of Dutch metal), old toothbrush, craft glue, angel, candle-holder and candle.

METHOD
1. Basecoat the entire piece with two coats of Pthalo Green and Green Oxide mix.

2. Using masking tape, mask off the two areas you have chosen for the marbling and spattering. Apply one coat of varnish to these areas.

3. Have crumpled foil or plastic ready. Apply a thick coat of Rich Gold to the area you are going to marble. Quickly lift off this paint with the crumpled foil or plastic, creating a speckled effect. The plastic will take off more paint than the foil, so please stop when you are happy with the effect.

4. As the straight column will be spattered, mask off the top and bottom in preparation for gold leafing. Refer to Gold leafing on page 30 and gold leaf the top and bottom.

5. Using plastic wrap, tightly wrap the plastic wrap over the gold leafing. I used plastic wrap here to mask off, so that the gold leafing does not pull off once the spattering is finished — masking tape might pull off the gold leafing. Now make a watery mix of the greens, the Yellow Oxide and Rich Gold with the old toothbrush and spatter

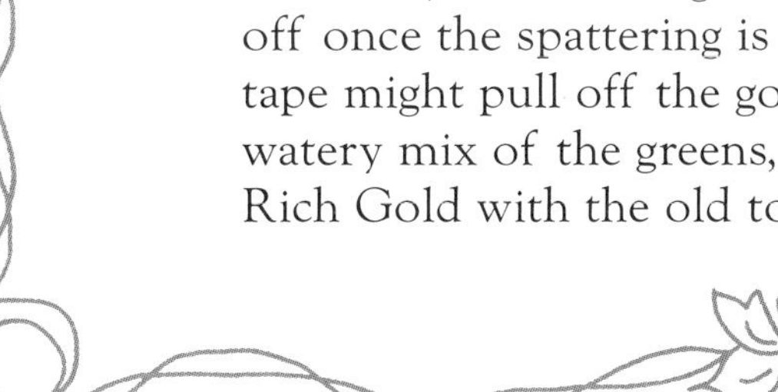
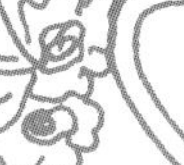
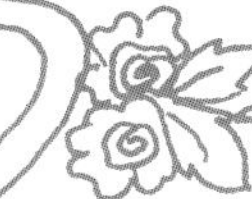

these colours on the area masked off previously, starting with the greens, then using the Yellow Oxide and Rich Gold. The spattering should be very fine and misty to contrast with the other areas.

6. Varnish the candleholder when dry, then glue on an angel. Purchase a suitable candle.

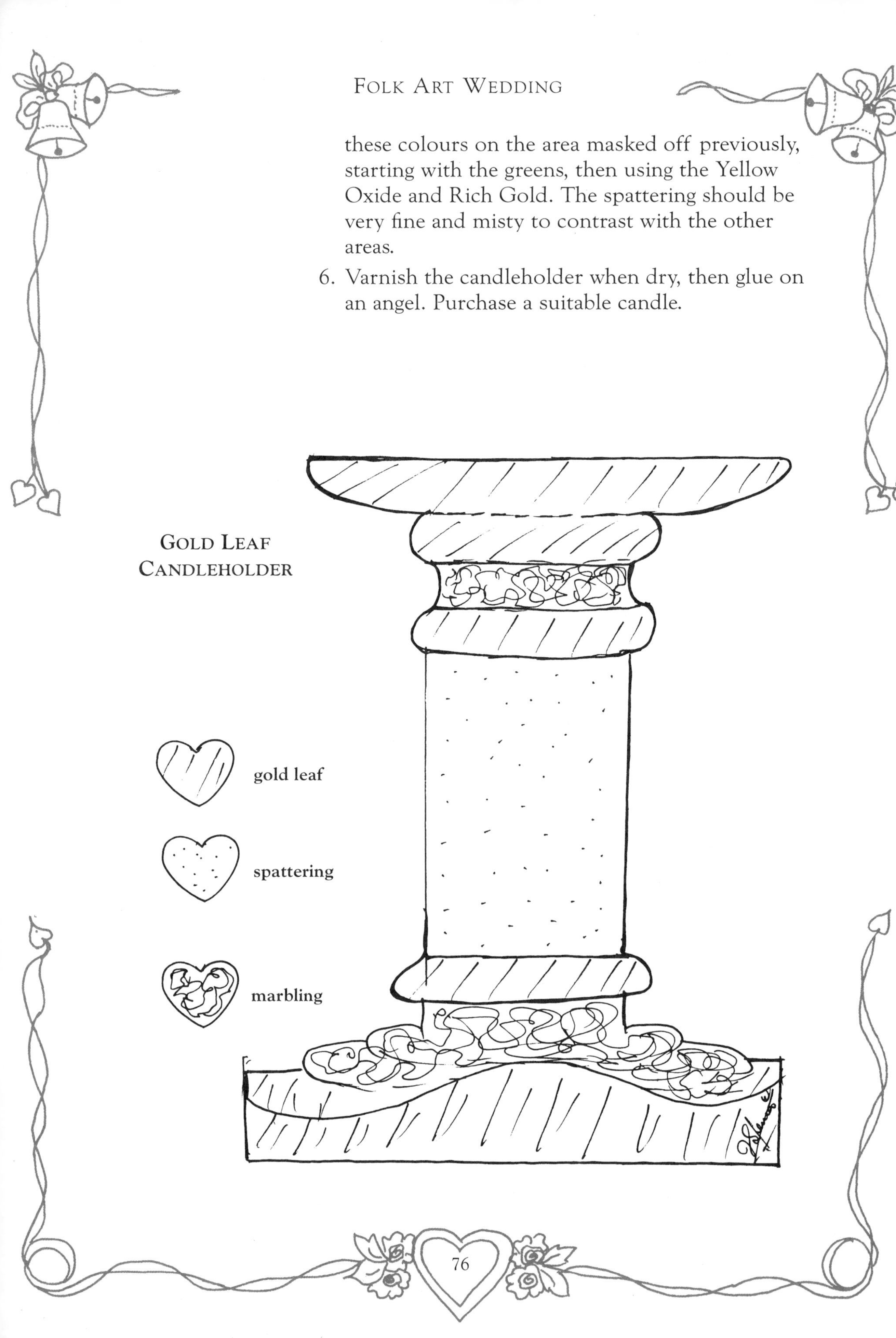

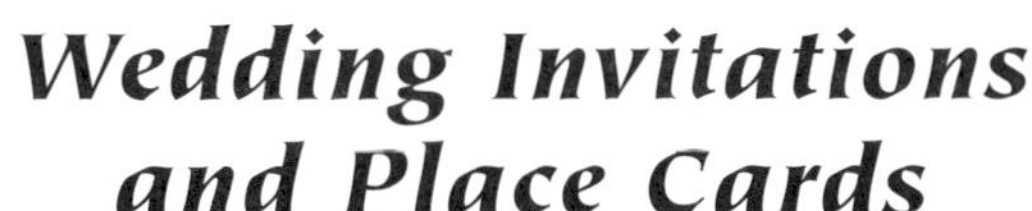

Wedding Invitations and Place Cards

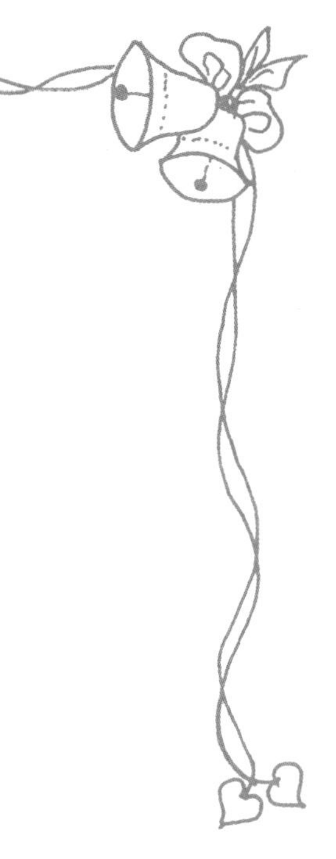

Each invitation is an A4 sheet of heavy paper similar to watercolour paper. The wording was chosen, then the invitations were printed. They were also cut and folded by the printer. The painting was done later.

Invitations of different shapes, sizes and colours are all possible, and I would refer you to my book *Folk Art Cards* for further ideas. You can use painting techniques that are small and dainty using the LAFS or ones that are larger and bolder, perhaps adapted from others in this book. Dimensional, metallic and glitter paints will add glamour to your invitations, place cards and 'thank you' cards after the wedding.

TECHNIQUES

Washes, LAFS, dagger leaves, flat brush blending, stencilling, lettering

COLOURS

Magenta, Teal Green, Green Oxide, Jade Green, Rich Gold

BRUSHES

No.3 round, fine liner, ⅛" dagger, small flat

OTHER MATERIALS

Gold pen

METHOD

1. Dilute Magenta with water and apply a small wash where the design will go.

2. Paint trails with the greens. (Refer to Light Airy Fairy Style on page 25.) Using Rich Gold and Teal Green, paint bows in the corner.

3. Add more Rich Gold and paint some small dagger leaves here and there.

4. Load your small flat brush with Magenta on one

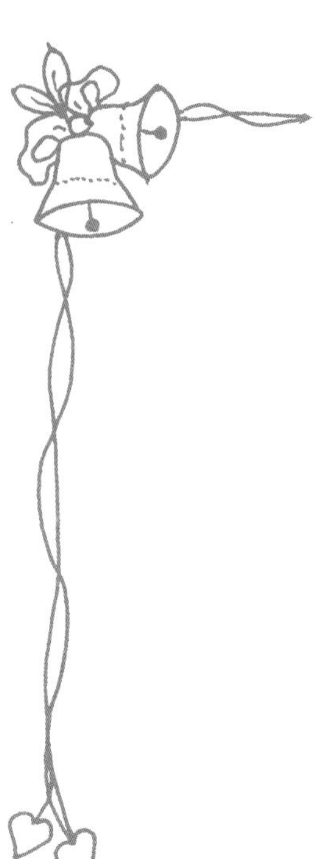

side and Rich Gold on the other and blend. With the gold on top pivot one petal. When dry pivot another petal. The flowers resemble small buds. (Refer to LAFS colour plate and to Flat Brush Blending on page 21.)

5. Paint the place cards and matching envelopes in the same manner. Gold or other coloured pens are available, and the writing of names and addresses could match the printing.

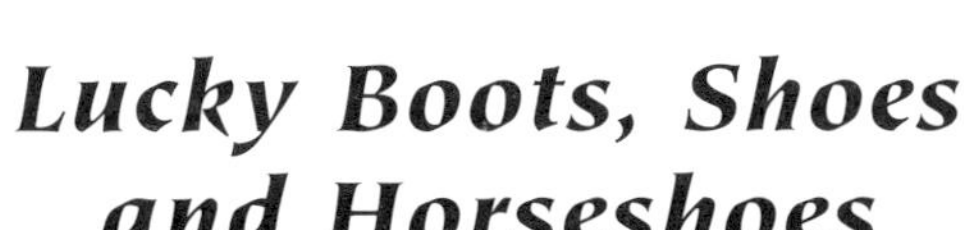

Lucky Boots, Shoes and Horseshoes

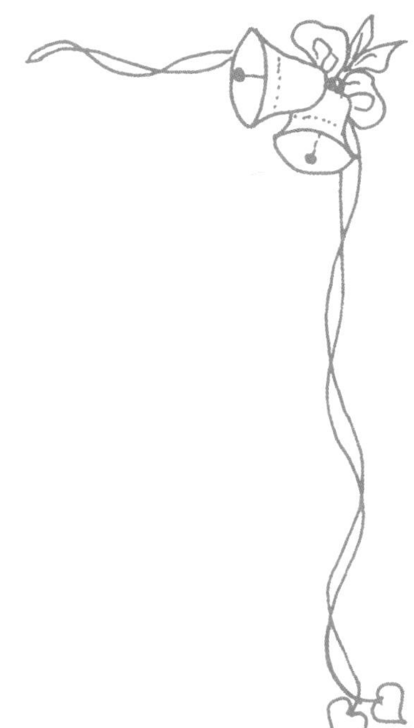

Traditionally, shoes are meant to bring good luck and fertility when thrown at the wedding couple. In a gentler interpretation of this custom, shoes and cans are tied onto the newlyweds' car, drawing attention to the happy couple as they drive away from the reception.

LUCKY BOOT

The old boot featured in the colour plate is painted blue and decorated with best wishes for the bride and groom written in gold paint. First, you will have to find an old boot, or someone else — maybe the bridesmaids, the best or a family member — might offer to do it for you. I found one boot only, in reasonable condition, at a Goodwill store.

TECHNIQUE
Lettering

COLOURS
Ultramarine, Iridescent Gold fabric paint

BRUSHES
Basecoater, No.3 round

OTHER MATERIALS
Wet and dry sandpaper, leather laces, thonging or ribbon

METHOD
1. Wash, dry and air the boot. Sand and apply two or more coats of Ultramarine.
2. Write your message with the Iridescent Gold paint nozzle.
3. Thread leather laces, thonging or ribbon through the holes.

Just Married

Joy   Health

Good Luck

Wealth

Happiness

Messages for Lucky Boot
and Champagne Slipper

PINK CHAMPAGNE SLIPPER

I thought pink champagne would go well with this shoe. I see no reason why the groom cannot drink from this slipper. You are creating new traditions and the painted shoe will be a wonderful treasure. In fact, if you painted two, you could wear them at your wedding.

This shoe is painted in the same manner as the Bride's Bath Box. It is marbled on the inner sole, the heel, the sole of the shoe and as a border around the base of the shoe's uppers. Leave a small white area on the sole of the shoe if you wish to add any writing in white dimensional paint.

TECHNIQUES

Marbling, LAFS, lettering with dimensional paint, washes

PINK CHAMPAGNE SLIPPER

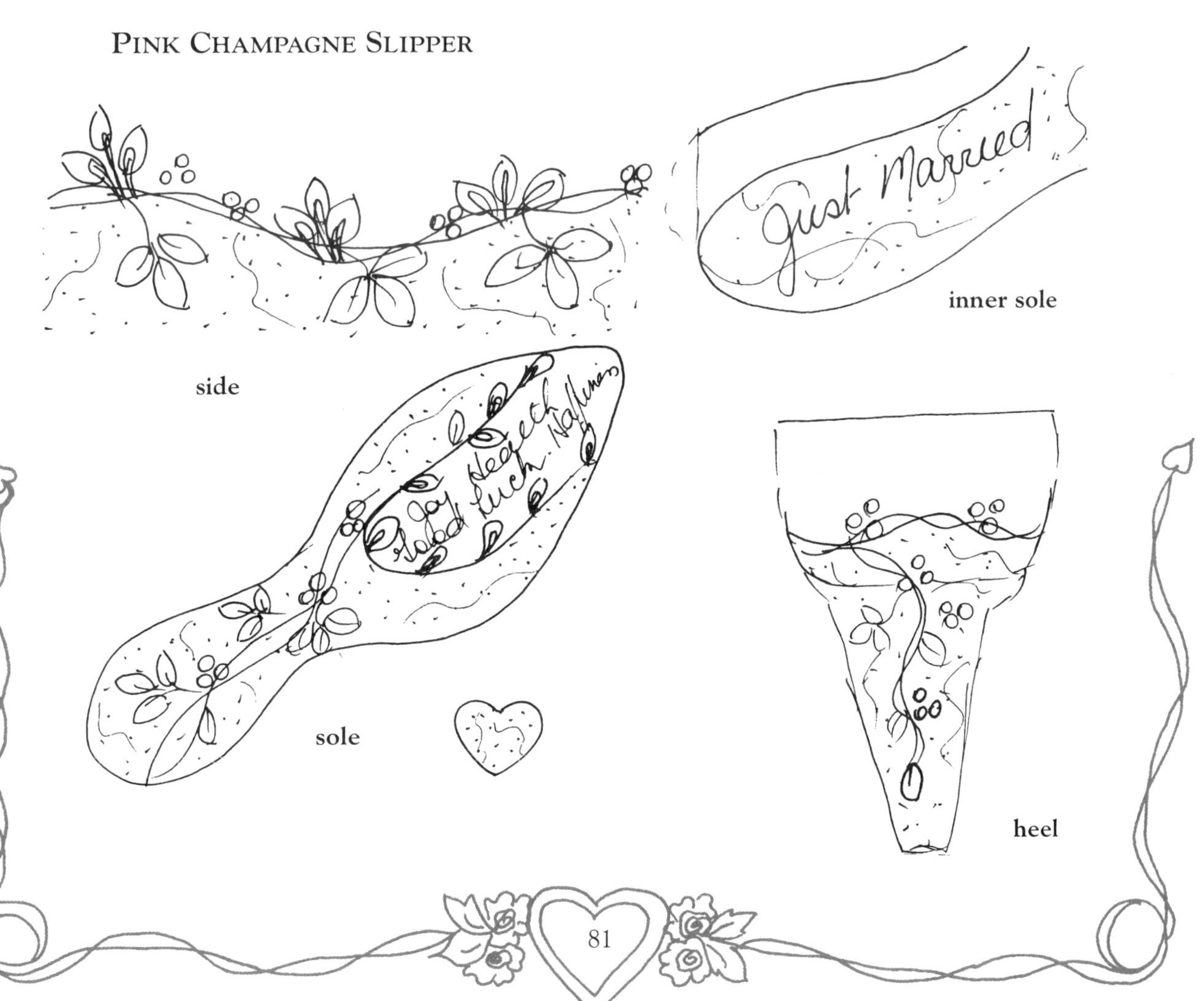

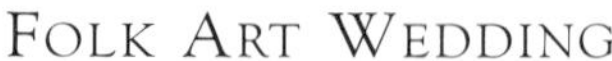
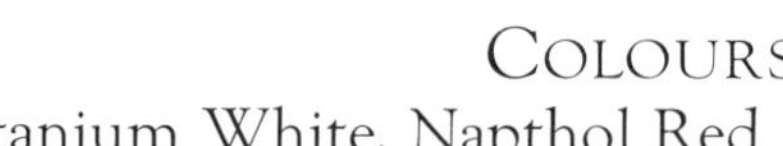

Colours

Titanium White, Napthol Red Light, Pink and White dimensional paint, White Pearl metallic.

Brushes

Basecoater, ⅛" dagger, fine liner, large round

Other Materials

Plastic wrap, small plastic cherub, craft glue

Method

1. Wash, dry and air the shoe, then apply two or three coats of Titanium White to the entire shoe.

2. Have the plastic wrap ready for marbling. Apply a pink mix of Napthol Red Light and Titanium White around the shoe and on the heel and dab with the plastic. Marble the inner sole and the sole of the shoe. Leave a small area white for writing if necessary.

3. Darken the pink mix a little for trails and leaves. Paint in the LAFS. Paint pink leaves on white and white leaves on pink, and paint veins and stems in the same way.

4. Using dimensional paints write 'Just Married' and the date inside the shoe, and 'Joy, Good Health, Happiness...' on the sole.

5. Basecoat the small cherub pink or white, then give it several water washes of darker pink. Finish with a White Pearl wash to obtain a pleasant effect and colour. Glue the cherub onto the shoe.

PAINTED SHOES TO MATCH THE BRIDAL TRAIN

I used a new pair of leather shoes, but cream satin shoes would also be suitable. Both can be painted with the same colours and paints. Folk art paint does not need the addition of a fabric or textile medium if it is to be used on leather. (Refer to the Painted Train instructions on page 101 and colour plate.)

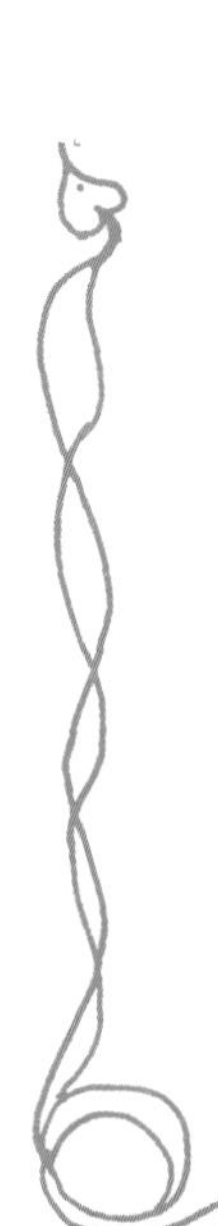

SHOES TO MATCH BRIDAL TRAIN

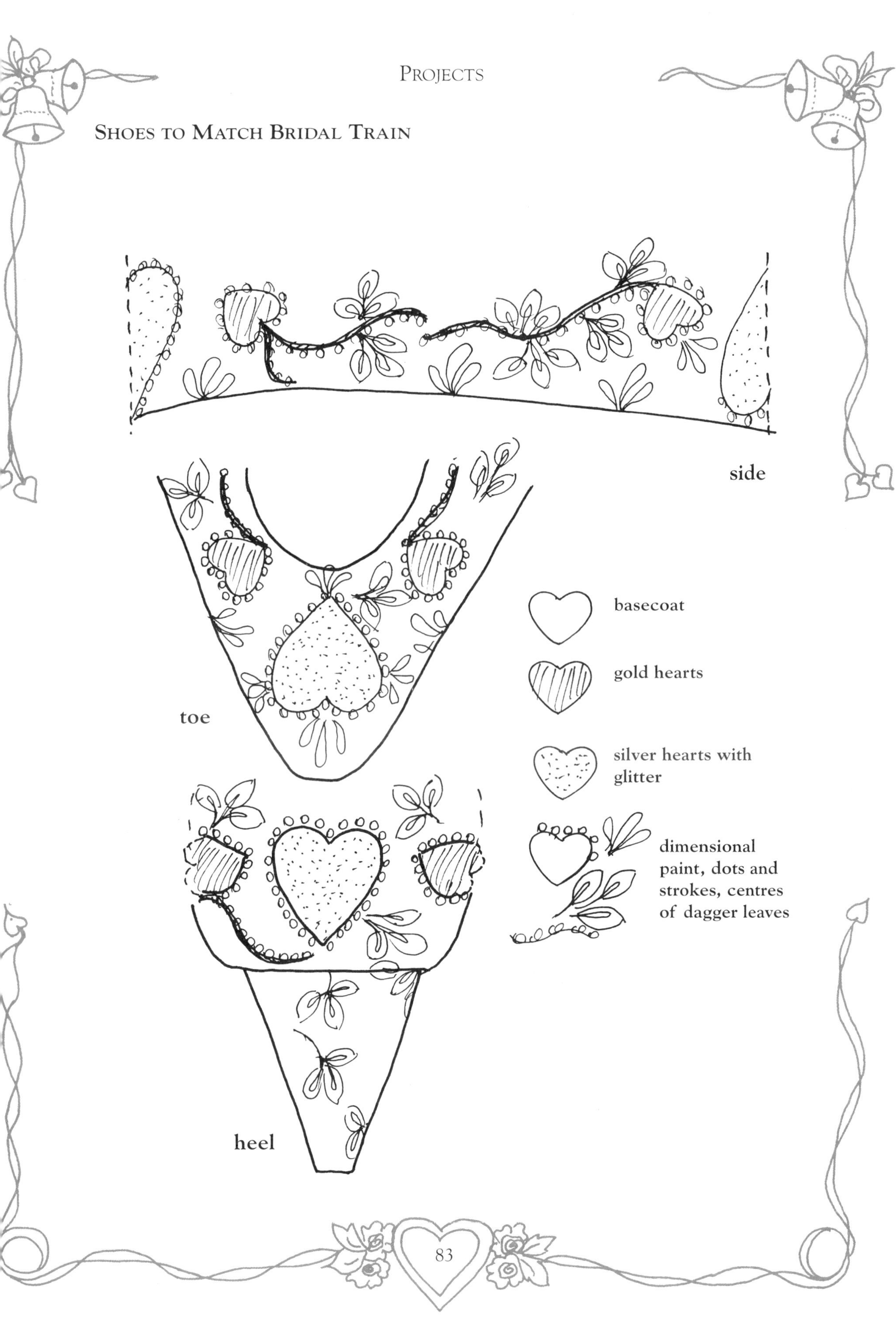

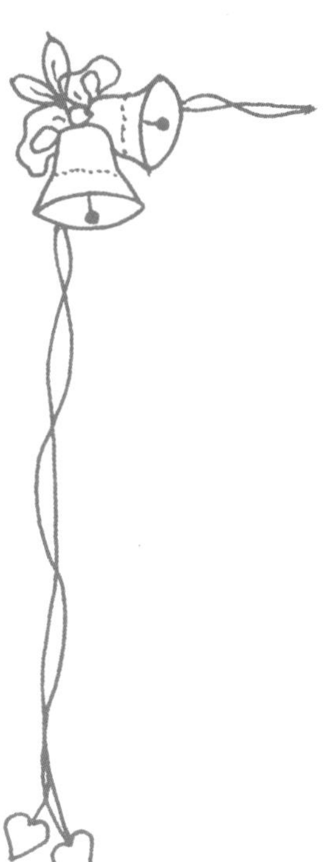

I found some small metal bows and thought that these would look great either glued or sewn onto the shoes. Perhaps one could be glued onto the heel. Small cherubs painted like the one on the Pink Champagne Slipper would also look elegant.

GOOD LUCK HORSESHOES

Once again, horseshoes are a sign of good luck, and are often hung on the bride's arm as she leaves the church. The horseshoe is supposed to hang up to keep in the luck, rather than hang down and let the luck run out. Craftwood horseshoes can be purchased from folk art and craft shops or can be cut out by a handyman.

As with pots and boxes, all techniques and colour schemes are possible on horseshoes. I have included two sizes for you and I painted them with the LAFS.

TECHNIQUES

LAFS

COLOURS

Any colours, including dimensional paints and metallics

BRUSHES

Fine liner, No.3 round, ⅛" flat shader or ¼" for larger roses.

OTHER MATERIALS

Ribbons, craft glue.

METHOD

1. Basecoat in the desired colour and then paint the design, keeping it simple. (Refer to Light Airy Fairy Style on page 25.) Suitable flowers are small or large roses

2. Glue on the ribbon to hang over the bride's arm, or decorate the shoes and use for pew decorations. (Refer to the colour plate.)

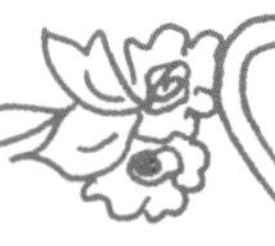

GOOD LUCK HORSESHOES (Actual size)

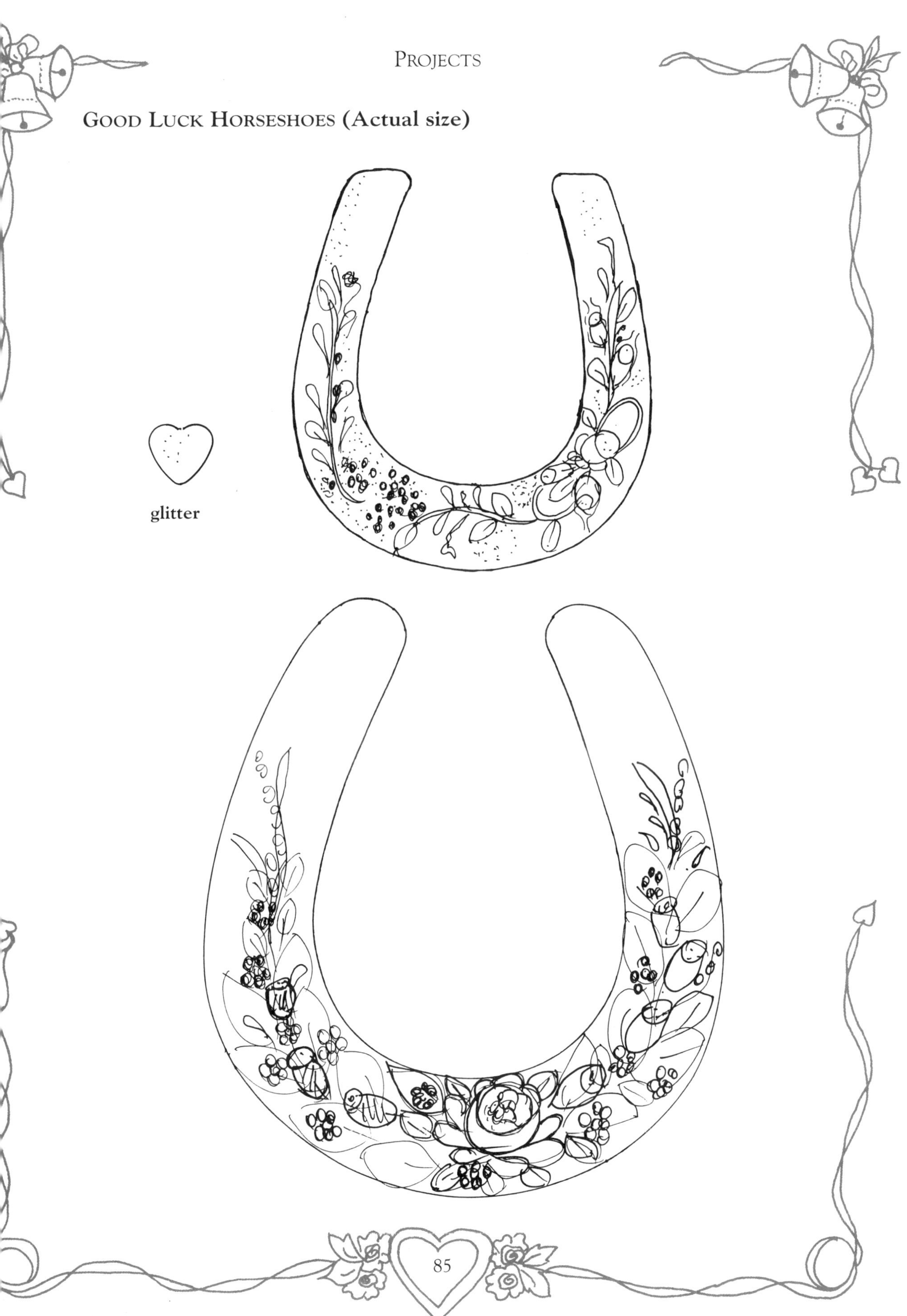

For the Cake

THE CAKE STAND

This stand was designed by a friend and wood-worker, who over the years has learnt to interpret my requests for certain items like this cake stand. 'You know, Don, a cake stand, some of your edges on it, the legs to go out, the cake will be oval, so could the stand be a rectangle? Something nice, please, it's for Llewellyn.' This is the cake stand that Don designed — I was thrilled with it. I could imagine it being very useful later on for Christmases, birthdays and christenings.

Instructions are given for a stand made from Craftwood.

TECHNIQUE

LAFS

COLOURS

Wicker White FolkArt spray paint (possibly 2 cans will be needed), Rich Gold, Ultramarine Blue, Titanium White

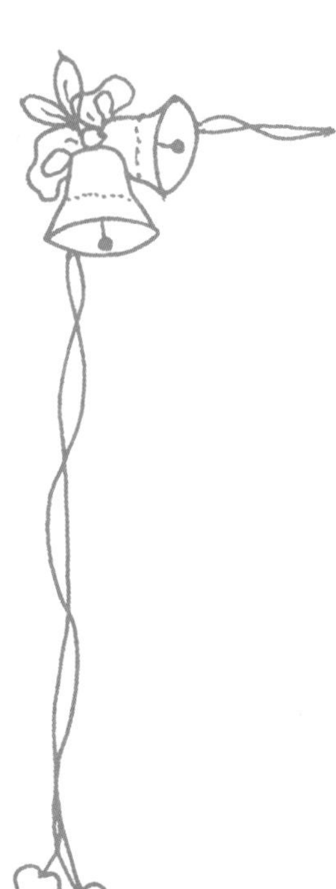

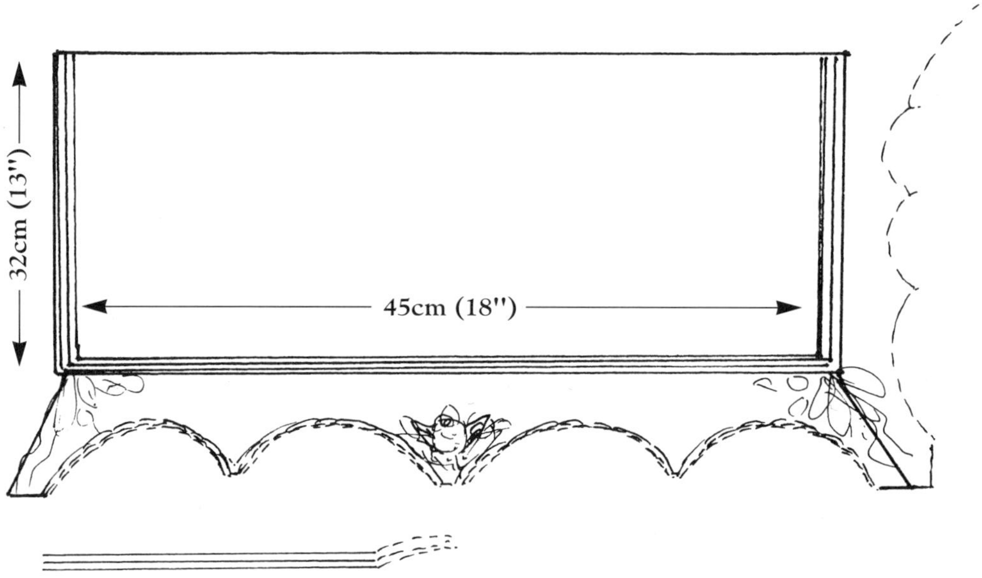

CAKE STAND

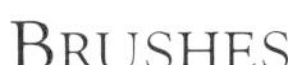

BRUSHES

No.5 round, fine liner, ⅛" dagger, No.4 or ⅛" flat, Cormack series 2930 No.6 wedge

OTHER MATERIALS

Wet and dry sandpaper, sealer (such as Jo Sonja's All Purpose Sealer), 4 small plastic cherubs, craft glue, semi-gloss or gloss FolkArt spray varnish

PREPARATION

1. Sand lightly. Fold the wet and dry paper and sand into the grooves left when the edges were routed. Seal. Sand lightly again if necessary.

2. The basecoat can be applied with a brush, but this is one instance where I used the FolkArt spray paint. Use Wicker White or the colour of your choice. (When painting large areas of gold I will basecoat first with one coat of Turner's Yellow, then apply 2 coats of Rich Gold for a good opaque coverage.) Please read labels and follow the spray instructions. I always spray outside on a table in the garden.

A professional finish is needed here, as the surface area is quite large and plain, so the underside needs to be painted too.

METHOD

1. Paint the routed edges and cherubs gold — at least three coats are needed. Glue on the cherubs.

2. Paint small trails, leaves and buds in Ultramarine Blue and Titanium White in each corner and on either side of the cherubs. (Refer to Light Airy Fairy Style on page 25 and the colour plate.) Paint small blue and white roses on each corner.

3. Paint bows on each corner — half the bow on one side and half the bow on the other side. The bows are made with the No.6 wedge. This brush has a three-sided metal ferrule and the synthetic bristles are angled. It is possible to pick up a different colour paint on each side of the brush. It

is a good idea to practise these bows on paper first. I like to stand up to paint these bows — I seem to get my arm flowing and be able to judge the pressure on the brush better. Make sure there is water in the brush, then pick up gold, blue and white paint.

With the brush loaded, go down with pressure and up with no pressure.

4. To make the trails of ribbons, go down with pressure, release the pressure to get a fine line, then apply more pressure to get a thicker line, finishing with a light wispy trail.

5. The final finish is a spray of varnish. This will give the cake stand a wipeable surface. It may be a good idea to always use a cake board in the future.

GRANNY'S OLD CHINA KNIFE

When cutting the cake, it is customary to use a good carving or cake knife, adorned with a bow. Rather than go to added expense, yet not liking the knife at the reception place, I painted the wooden handle of a bread knife, found on one of my market jaunts. Old knives are not hard to find.

This lovely cake knife will match the cake stand you are going to paint.

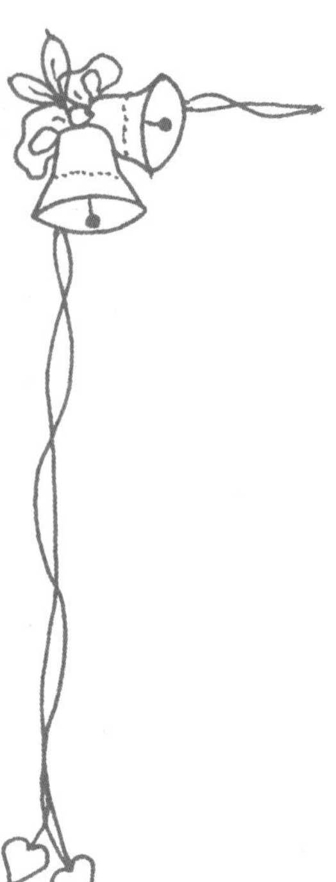

GRANNY'S OLD
CHINA KNIFE

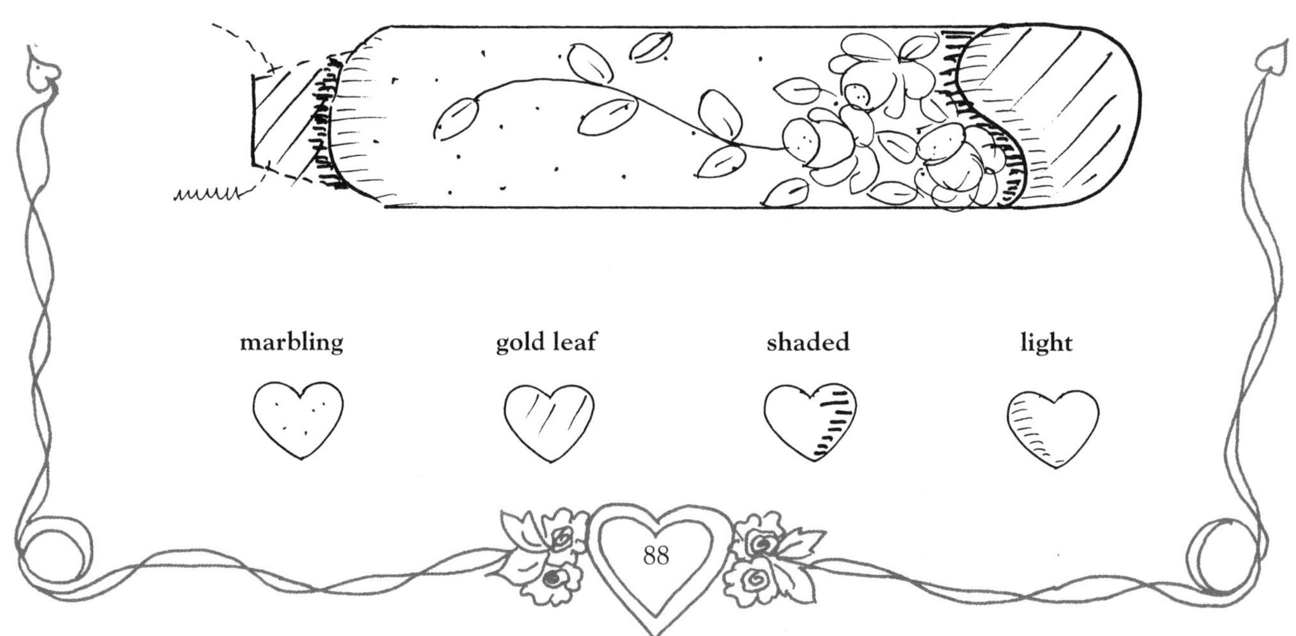

Techniques

Marbling, dry brushing, LAFS, dagger leaves, flat brush blending

Colours

Ultramarine Blue, Rich Gold, Pale Gold, Warm White, Storm Blue

Brushes

1" Basecoater, No.3 round, fine liner, ¼" dagger, ⅛" flat

Other Materials

Wet and dry sandpaper, Kleister medium, plastic bag, water-based gloss varnish.

Method

1. Sand the handle, clean the blade and wash the knife well if old. Basecoat Ultramarine Blue (three coats), then Rich Gold (three coats) where illustrated.

2. When dry, mix equal parts of Pale Gold and Kleister medium, and paint the blue-painted areas with this mix. Have the plastic bag ready and place it over the handle and roll the handle round and round. Have a look and see if you like the textured look. Most of the gold should have been removed, and the gold remaining should have a fine-veined look. Dry well.

3. Dry brush a little Pale Gold over the Rich Gold areas here and there.

4. Mix a little Warm White with Pale Gold and make a highlight area around where the Rich Gold meets the blue. Paint a narrow line with Storm Blue under the Rich Gold. This shadow line and highlight line is an attempt to make the handle appear to have a gold top and base.

5. Paint the small design down the handle with Warm White, Storm Blue and Ultramarine Blue. (Refer to Light Airy Fairy Style on page 25 and the colour plate.) Paint in the LAFS and include

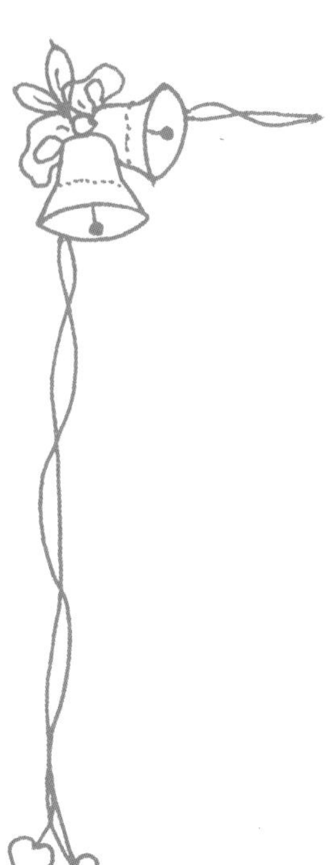

some dagger leaves. With the ⅛" flat brush paint some small roses here and there. (Refer to Flat Brush Blending on page 21.)

6. Apply several coats of varnish to the handle. A high-gloss look will give a glazed china appearance.

BLUE AND GOLD STRAWBERRY CAKE TRAY

I painted these trays using the blue, gold and white colour scheme of the wedding. They were used to carry the cut cake in packets to the guests, and then were given away to the lucky guests named on the back of the place-cards. Two or more trays may be needed.

TECHNIQUES
LAFS, dagger leaves, liner work, round brush blending, dry brushing, dots, double-loaded strokes, flat brush work, comma strokes

COLOURS
Ultramarine Blue, Blue Sapphire metallic, Rich Gold, Pearl White, Pale Gold, Storm Blue, Warm White

BRUSHES
1" Basecoater, ¼" and ⅛" dagger, fine liner, No.3 round, ⅛" flat

OTHER MATERIALS
Paper towels, stylus, sealer, water-based varnish

METHOD

1. Lightly sand the tray and seal to make the basecoat grab the surface. Basecoat in Ultramarine Blue or colour of your choice. Then apply two coats of Blue Sapphire metallic.

2. Apply two or three coats of Rich Gold to the centre of the tray, painting an irregular outline rather than just a circle.

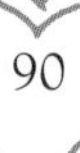

**BLUE AND GOLD
STRAWBERRY
CAKE TRAY**

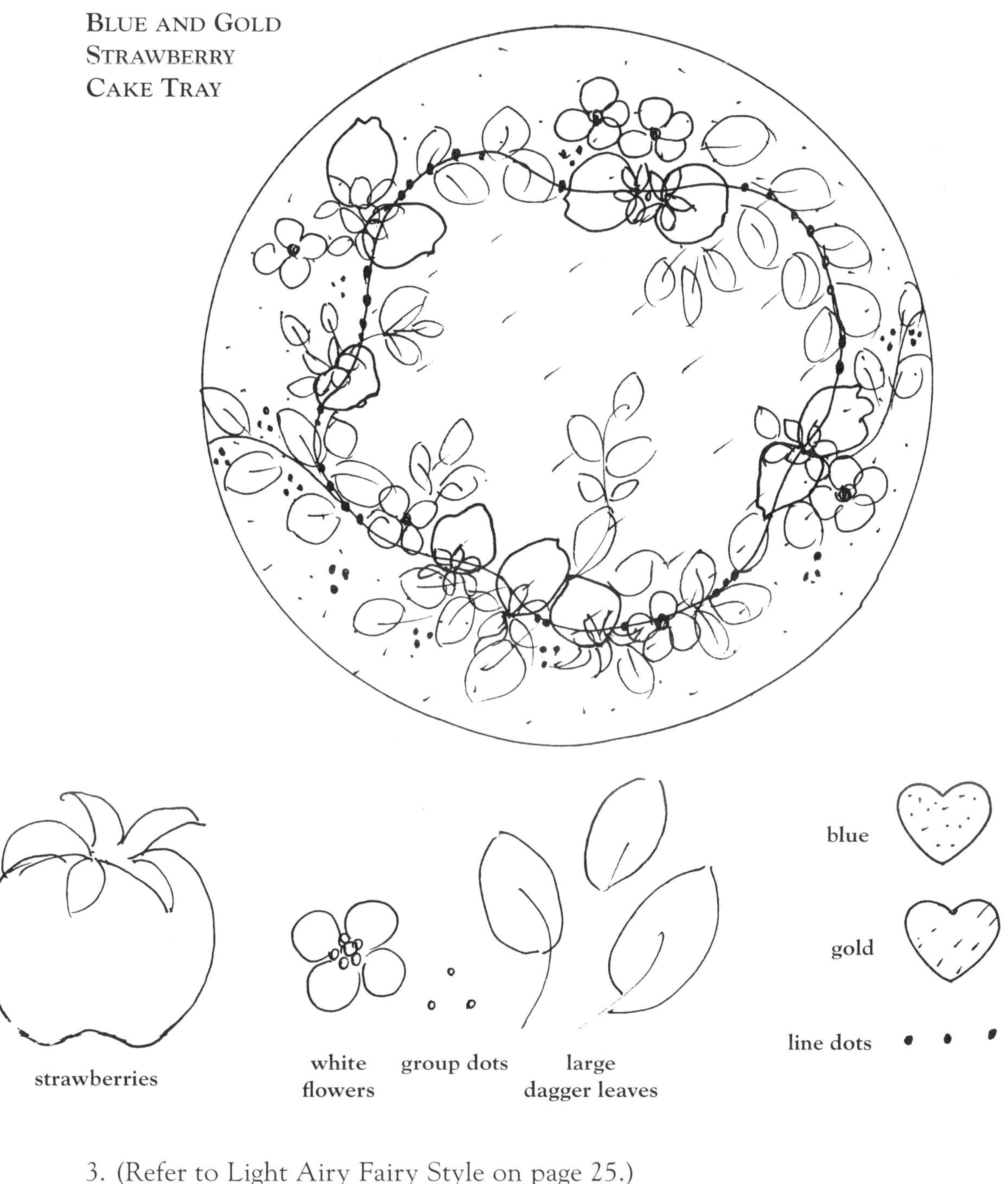

3. (Refer to Light Airy Fairy Style on page 25.)
   Paint trails and groups of leaves using the larger
   dagger brush and diluted Pearl White, Rich and
   Pale Gold. Using the smaller dagger brush and
   the same colours, paint some little leaves here
   and there. With the liner brush add veins of

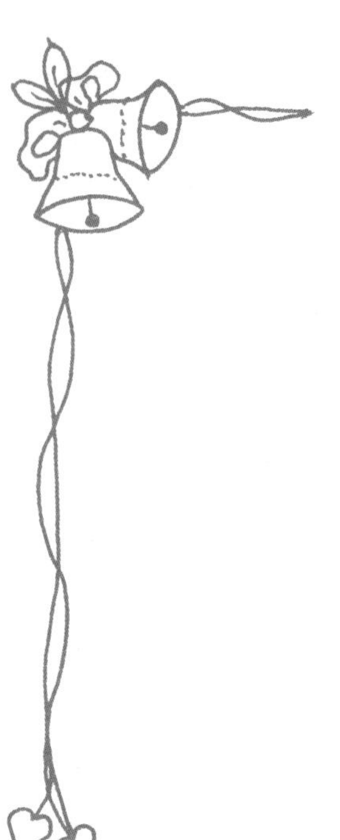

Storm Blue, Warm White and gold to the leaves.

4. Trace or freehand some strawberries, going in different directions. Reduce the size if preferred. (I painted mine large so that you could see the blended technique.)

5. Basecoat the strawberries with two coats of Ultramarine Blue.

6. Referring to Round Brush Blending on page 20 and the colour plate, paint the strawberries. Highlight with dry brushing and white dots.

7. Paint double-loaded strokes of gold and white on the tops of the berries. (Refer to Double-Loaded Strokes on page 19.)

8. Pick up some white paint in the small flat brush and blend into the brush all the way across to make the white four-petalled flowers and one-petal buds. The stroke is a pivot. Repeat the blending. If desired you can pick up a little gold on one corner of the brush and put the gold on the bottom and white on the top. Put gold dots in the centres of the white flowers. The small buds have a gold comma stroke for a vein and stem. (Refer to Round Brush Blending on page 20 and Comma Strokes on page 18.)

9. With a stylus, apply groups of gold dots here and there beside the leaves, and outline the centre border with gold dots where there is no painting.

10. Finish with two coats of varnish.

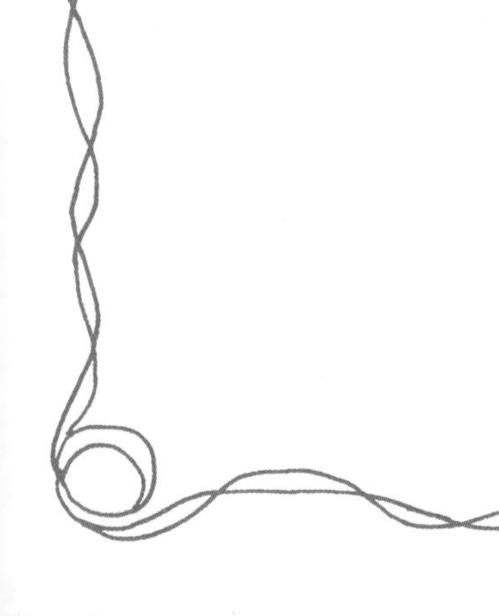

Frames and More Frames

OLD SILVER FRAME

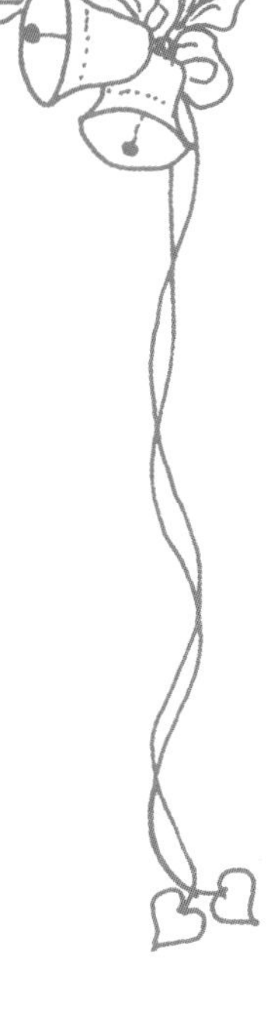

A handpainted photo frame containing the wedding photo would make a great gift for a close relative or friend who is unable to attend the wedding. An old family photo would also look wonderful in this frame.

Most of the techniques in this book can be applied to frames, particularly the LAFS or marbling, but I wanted to do something very different for you.

The following instructions are for a silver-leafed and antiqued frame, but it is up to you whether you silver leaf and antique the frame or not, otherwise use silver paint. (For example, this frame would look effective painted with ivory, rather than silver leafed, and then antiqued.) If you do decide to silver leaf your frame, remember that the plainer the frame, the easier it is to leaf. We all see colour differently, so if you are not happy with any colour or effect, please use your own colours.

The coloured matting that is obtainable from most print-developing shops and which fits most frames will set off your photo beautifully.

TECHNIQUES
Silver leafing, antiquing

COLOURS
Ultramarine Blue, Silver, Silver or Pearl dimensional paint, Rich Gold

BRUSHES
Large basecoater, large round

OTHER MATERIALS
Wet and dry sandpaper, sealer (such as Jo Sonja's All Purpose Sealer),

1 m of silver cord, packet of pearls (from craft shops), small packets of assorted plastic leaves

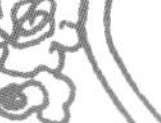
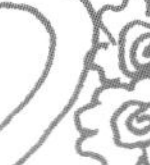

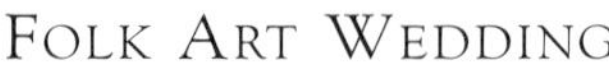

and beads (from craft shops or supermarkets), small metal cherubs (from craft shops), clear craft glue or glue gun, silver leafing materials (see page 32 — you will need at least 6 sheets of silver leaf or a whole book), antiquing materials (see page 39)

Preparation

The plain wooden frame I purchased had a very smooth varnished surface, so it needed sanding to remove some of the slickness, and sealing to make the blue basecoat adhere. Take the frame apart and set the glass safely aside until you are ready to insert the photo.

Method

1. Apply two coats of Ultramarine Blue to the front and back of the frame. Apply two coats of Silver paint to the back of the frame.

2. Set out the cord, pearls, plastic and metal shapes and glue into position. After gluing the pearls, run some dimensional paint around them, so that they appear to be 'set'. Fill in any gaps with this paint, and add some small hearts and leaves as fillers here and there. Allow at least 24 hours for the frame to dry.

3. Now the silver leafing (see page 32). When applying the tannin blocking sealer, make sure you get it in all the little cracks and crevices among the cord and shapes. Do not put sealer over the pearls. You can cut the sheets in small pieces and place more leaf over the leaves, beads and pearls, as you want a good coverage.

4. If there are any blue areas, retouch them with Silver. Dry brush a little Silver over this.

5. You may wish to stop here, but I went on to antique my frame. Leave the dark mixture mostly around the glued areas, leaving the top silver looking. The pearls do not want to be too shiny.

6. When dry, dry brush the little Rich Gold very

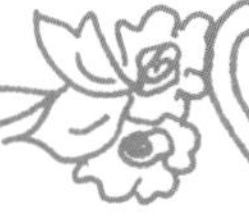

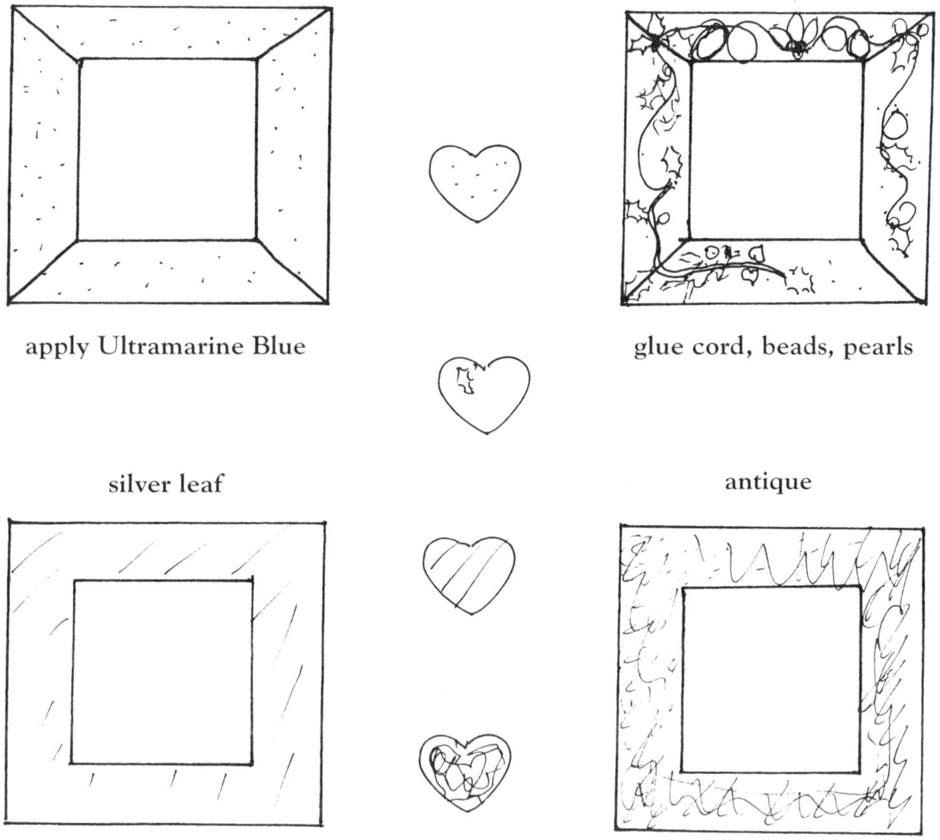

apply Ultramarine Blue

glue cord, beads, pearls

silver leaf

antique

lightly onto some of the raised areas, such as the leaves, so that the frame resembles old worn silver.

7. Apply two coats of varnish.

OLD SILVER FRAME

THE GOLD, PEARL AND PEWTER FRAME

This frame makes a perfect setting for that special photo. If you are unable to find this shape, trace the frame and have one made in craftwood, or adjust the silver design to another shape. The pearl hearts are found in most craft shops and larger fabric shops.

TECHNIQUES
Dry brushing, antiquing

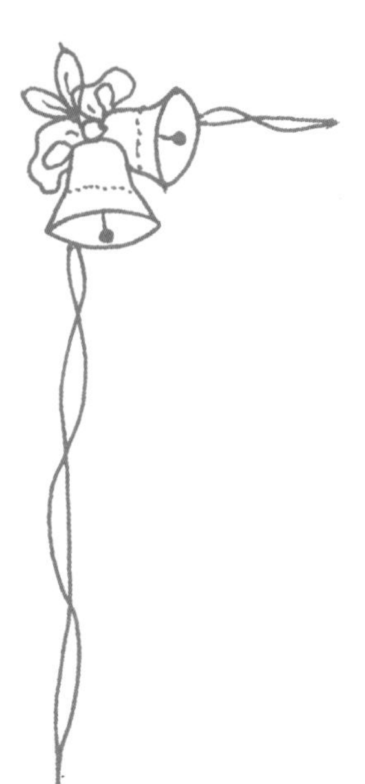

COLOURS

Rich Gold, Pale Gold, Silver Colourpoint dimensional paint

BRUSHES

Large basecoater, large round

OTHER MATERIALS

Wet and dry sandpaper, sealer (such as Jo Sonja's All Purpose Sealer), antiquing materials (see page 39), cotton bud, pearl hearts in assorted sizes, stylus or toothpick, clear craft glue

METHOD

1. Sand, seal then basecoat the entire frame with two or more coats of Rich Gold.

2. Sand lightly and dry brush a little Pale Gold towards the edges of the frame. Because this frame was made of timber and not craftwood, the grain of the timber lends itself to dry brushing, with the colours settling into the grooves.

3. Trace the silver or pewter design, and fill in with the dimensional paint. Smooth with a brush. If two coats are needed, dry the first coat overnight.

4. Refer to the Colour Plate and note that some small holes were punched with a stylus or toothpick into the silver paint to achieve a more realistic handmade pewter effect. Also, when the silver is antiqued, these little holes fill with the antique medium and show up better.

5. Carefully and lightly antique the silver, using a cotton bud. (Refer to Antiquing on page 39.)

6. Glue on the pearl hearts.

GRANITE PHOTO FRAME (OR IS IT?)

No, they are very cheap clear plastic frames, quickly spattered with different colours to resemble stone — and very expensive photo frame. I found the

GOLD, PEARL AND PEWTER FRAME

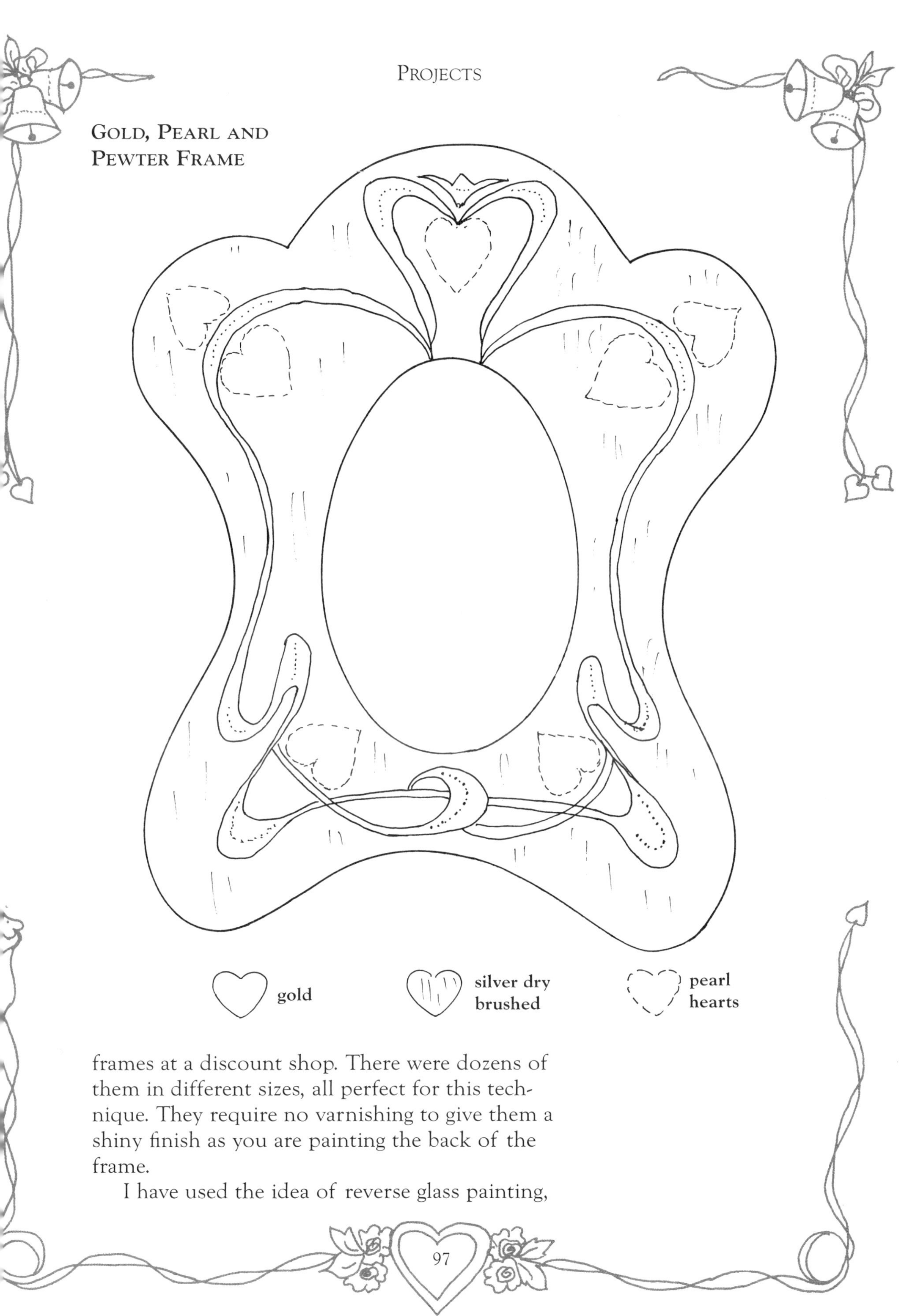

frames at a discount shop. There were dozens of them in different sizes, all perfect for this technique. They require no varnishing to give them a shiny finish as you are painting the back of the frame.

I have used the idea of reverse glass painting,

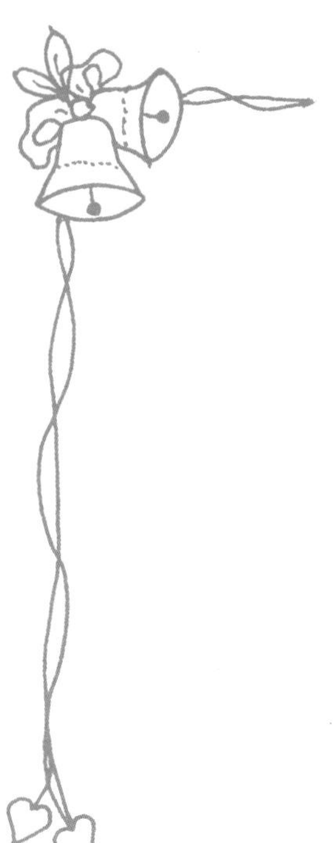

which is an old European technique. The first colour you see (the top colour) is painted first. For instance, if you were painting a leaf, you would paint the veins first, then the light and shading, then the leaf colour at the back.

These simple frames, each containing your wedding photo, could be given to the female guests. They would be great for an assembly line production. The children could help too.

I heard of a wedding where a photo was taken of the bride and groom, the film was rushed to a photo print shop, dozens of the prints were developed, and every guest received a copy of the photo at the reception. What if they were put in a spattered frame? Sensational!

Technique

Spattering

Colours

Warm White, Pale Gold, Pale Pink, Burgundy (or assorted colours to complement your photo), Black

Brushes

Large basecoater

Other Materials

Newspaper, old toothbrush, hair dryer

Method

1. Spread out the newspaper. Mix the paints and spatter on the back of the frame in the following order (working from light to dark): Warm White, Pale Gold, Pale Pink mixing to darker pinks, Burgundy and Black. Spatter on the back of the frame only. Dry between spatter colours with the hair dryer.

2. When dry, and you like the effect, paint a coat of black paint over your beautiful spattering. Now just turn the frame over, and you have a marvellous plastic gloss finish that would normally require hours of varnishing.

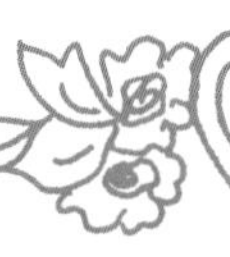

Coathangers

These wooden hangers are most useful for the bride or bridesmaid's gown. With basic painting skills and imagination, your whole wardrobe could be full of your hand-painted dress hangers. The hangers are available from supermarkets. Other suitable hangers are wooden skirt and trouser hangers — his and hers!

TECHNIQUES
Stencilling or tracing, LAFS, double-loaded strokes, dots, commas strokes, cross-hatching, lettering

COLOURS
Warm White, Purple, Green Oxide, Rich Gold, Yellow Oxide, Napthol Red Light

BRUSHES
Basecoater, No.3 round, fine liner

OTHER MATERIALS
Heart stencil, paper towels, stylus, tracing equipment (see page 35), water-based varnish, ribbon

METHOD

1. Apply three coats of Ivory basecoat to the front and back, support and hook. Sand well between coats. Apply three coats of Rich Gold around the outside edges of the coathanger.

2. Trace or stencil the heart and basecoat with a pale mauve mix of Warm White and Purple.

3. Paint some LAFS trails with Green Oxide. Paint some green hearts leaves here and there. (Refer to colour plate.) When dry, shade and highlight the leaves as shown. Outline with Rich Gold and connect to the stems.

4. To paint violets, pick up some Purple or mauve mix with your round brush and tip into Warm White. Make double-loaded strokes — two at the top and one on either side — then pull three

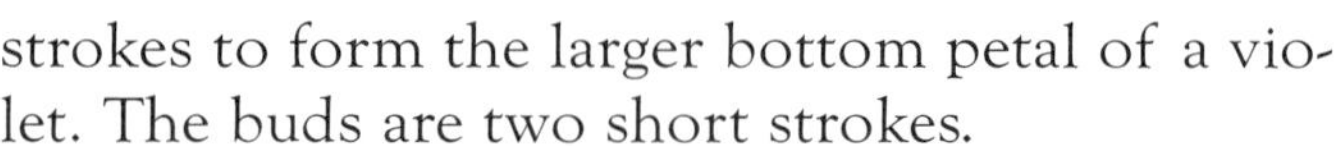

strokes to form the larger bottom petal of a violet. The buds are two short strokes.

5. Make a small Yellow Oxide dot with a stylus in the centre of each violet. Mix Napthol Red Light and Yellow Oxide to make orange, and pull a comma stroke with the stylus each side of the yellow dot.

6. Connect the buds and violets to the main stem with Green Oxide, and paint small side leaves for the buds.

7. With the fine liner brush and Warm White diluted with a little water, cross-hatch the hearts. (Cross-hatching is painting thin lines diagonally across the design or shape in one direction and then painting thin lines in the opposite direction, creating diamond shapes.) Apply groups of three dots of Rich Gold in any gaps with a stylus.

8. Select the initials if desired and trace them on. Apply three coats of Rich Gold. When dry, erase all graphite lines.

9. Tie a small bow of ribbon onto the hook.

COATHANGER

Painted Train

This fabulous painted train will add the finishing touch to your gown, creating wonderful back interest as you float up and down the aisle.

It is not hard to paint, although it will take time and requires co-operation between the designer, painter and dressmaker. For example, if the pattern calls for a train built into the dress, you will have to cut the material and paint it before giving it to the dressmaker.

If there is more than one painter, it is a great help if they sit side by side or opposite each other at the table or board. It is also a good idea for them to paint a sample of the design on paper so that any differences in their painting styles (some painters cannot paint freehand, or their paint mixture is thicker or thinner) are noted early. These differences can then be ironed out before commencing the train. The other way to go is to commission a folk painter to paint your train.

Painting on other parts of the dress — such as bows, folds, sleeves, collars — would look superb too. You can also paint parts of your wedding attendants' dresses.

If you are doing the painting yourself, choose a suitable place to paint, where the fabric can be left flat and safe from prying eyes. I painted the train on the dining-room table. Underneath my length of fabric I placed some plastic, old sheeting and cotton lining to absorb excess paint. I placed a folded towel where I was painting. I used a foam tray to hold brushes and paint, and placed only a little water in my jar at any one time and changed it frequently, just in case of a spillage. Keep your hands clean, ensure that you have good lighting and keep your interpretation of the design handy, and you will create a wonderful masterpiece and a family treasure.

TECHNIQUES
Stencilling, LAFS, liner work, dagger leaves

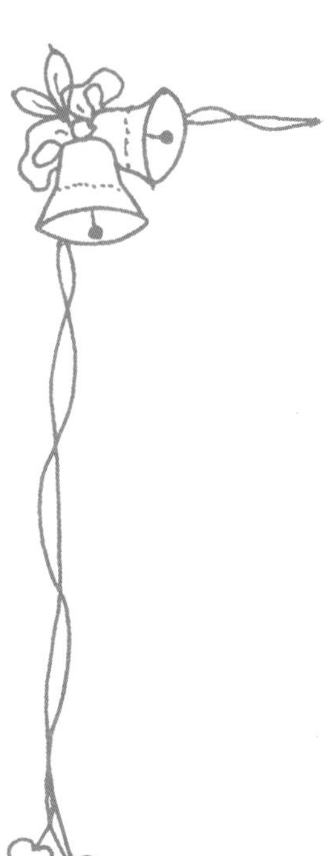

Colours

Fabric paints, dimensional paints and FolkArt paints mixed with a textile medium are used. Read all labels, and if the paint needs 72 hours to mature, then please allow that time.

Acrylic paints:

FolkArt Ivory, Duncan Pearl Mystical Silver, Jo Sonja's Rich Gold and Textile Medium.

Dimensional paints:

Fashion Show Pearl Champagne, Duncan Scribblers, Iridescent Light Gold, Colourpoint Ivory Pearl Paint Stitching

Glitter paints:

Derivan Glitz a Matazz Crystal, Duncan Sparklers and Glittering Crystal, Fashion Show Rainbow Glitter

Brushes

Old short-haired brush for stencilling (I used a ¼" Tacklon flat brush), line 00, Nos 3 and 5 round, ⅛" and ¼" dagger

Fabric

For my design I used 2 m of plain cream polyester silk. You will, of course, use your chosen wedding material and pattern. Remember that the material used for the train need not be the same as that for the dress. If you are having a lace dress, then a satin or silk train would provide a lovely contrast. Please paint a small sample of your chosen fabric beforehand, to check for paint adhesion and suitability. On some extremely light materials, the colour may bleed a little, although you might like this effect.

Other Materials

Transfer marking pencil or carbothello pencil, bow and angel stencils (from party shops and all department stores at Christmas), textile medium (mixed with the Ivory basecoat and the Rich Gold), Plaid 28311 small heart stencil, Plaid 28907 large heart flowers stencils (from craft shops), hair dryer

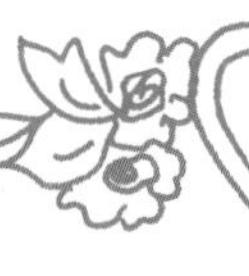

PREPARATION

Before commencing to paint, even the sample, read all the information and instructions thoroughly.

1. Pre-wash the fabric, drip dry, iron out all creases and roll around a cardboard cylinder.

2. Paint a sample.

3. Measure and mark where the designs will go. The design does not have to be the same as mine — you might settle for less painting. Do not put pins into the body of the fabric, just around the edges, and use transfer marking pencils which fade, or just dots with a carbothello pencil, which can be brushed or lightly wiped off.

4. Cut out stencils from large sheet

METHOD

Please refer frequently to the colour plate.

1. Mix a quantity of Ivory with the textile medium and put in a small jar. Position the stencils and paint the bows then the angels in this mixture. Retouch and give another coat if necessary.

2. Paint trails between the bows and angels using Ivory and the liner brush. Paint the ribbons from each side of the bow, with Ivory and the No.5 round brush. You may need to apply two coats.

3. Overpaint the bows and angels with Pearl Champagne. It glows.

4. Stencil the heart flowers with Mystical Silver. Apply two coats, the second coat with the No.5 round brush.

5. Using the ⅛" dagger brush, paint groups of three dagger leaves up and down the trails and around the bows, angels and heart flowers with the Pearl Champagne. Paint more groups of leaves with Mystical Silver. Paints small veins and stems on the leaves — Rich Gold on the Pearl Champagne, and Ivory on the Mystical Silver. These leaves are very pale, but they are part of the background design and shimmer when the light catches them.

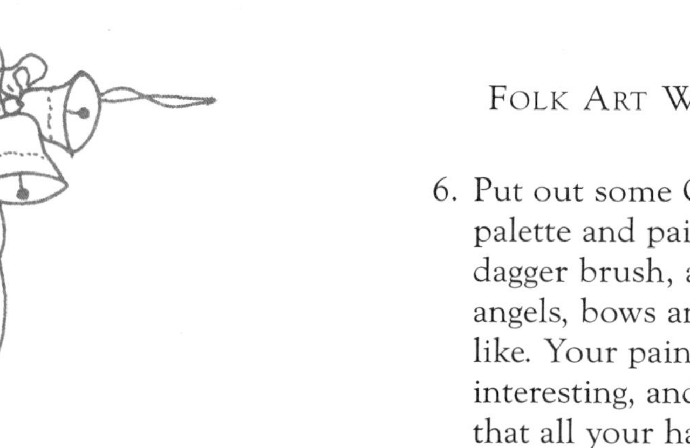

6. Put out some Glitz a Mattaz Crystal on your palette and paint groups of leaves with your ¼" dagger brush, all around your design, around the angels, bows and trails — in fact, anywhere you like. Your painting is now starting to look very interesting, and you are probably starting to feel that all your hard work is worth it. Remember that this glitter is an adhesive and will take time to dry, so work in one area at a time and then move along.

7. With the fine liner brush, paint fine veins and stems from the Glitz a Mattaz leaves with Ivory. Just quick fine painting, pointing the stems in the direction of the trails or bows or wherever you have painted them.

8. Paint some tendrils or decorative lines near the heart flowers with Ivory. (Refer to the colour plate.)

9. With the No.3 round brush, paint all the heart flowers and centres with Glitz a Mattaz Crystal, two coats if necessary.

10. Paint groups of small Rich Gold dagger leaves here and there — just a few. Paint the veins and stems with Ivory.

11. Stencil small gold hearts here and there around the design. I used a small plastic stencil cut from a larger stencil design. (Refer to Stencilling on page 33.) The Rich Gold may need two coats, but the second one can be painted on with a round brush.

12. When dry, apply the Duncan Glittering Crystal. Again, two coats may be needed.

13. Apply small strokes out from the top of the heart with the tip of the Scribblers Iridescent Light Gold.

14. Give the angels two coats of the Duncan Glittering Crystal. Apply the glitter thickly on the wings with the No.5 round brush, making strokes to resemble folds or feathers.

15. Go carefully and evenly and outline the edges of

the bows, the ribbons, the heart flowers and angels with the Ivory Pearl Colourpoint. Gently squeeze and lift the tip for each bead. A small peak is made which will soon settle into a lovely pearl bead. This 'Paint Stitching' as the product is called, comes in different colours such as gold. On the angels make an extra row of beads on the wings and hem of the dress. These beads seem to tie the design together, making your exquisite train look very romantic.

16. Dry all painting thoroughly, allowing three days for paints to cure. Blow drying with a hair dryer on a hot setting all over the train 'heat sets' the paint. Do not iron over your painting, but roll up the cotton lining and the painted train together around a cardboard cylinder from the fabric shop, and carry to the dressmaker like this. Place a few pins at the top, near the edges, to prevent the train from sliding down the cylinder.

Well done. You should be very proud of yourself. Do not be modest, tell yourself how clever you are. It will, however, be very hard to keep this a secret until the big day.

Painted Train — Suggested Design

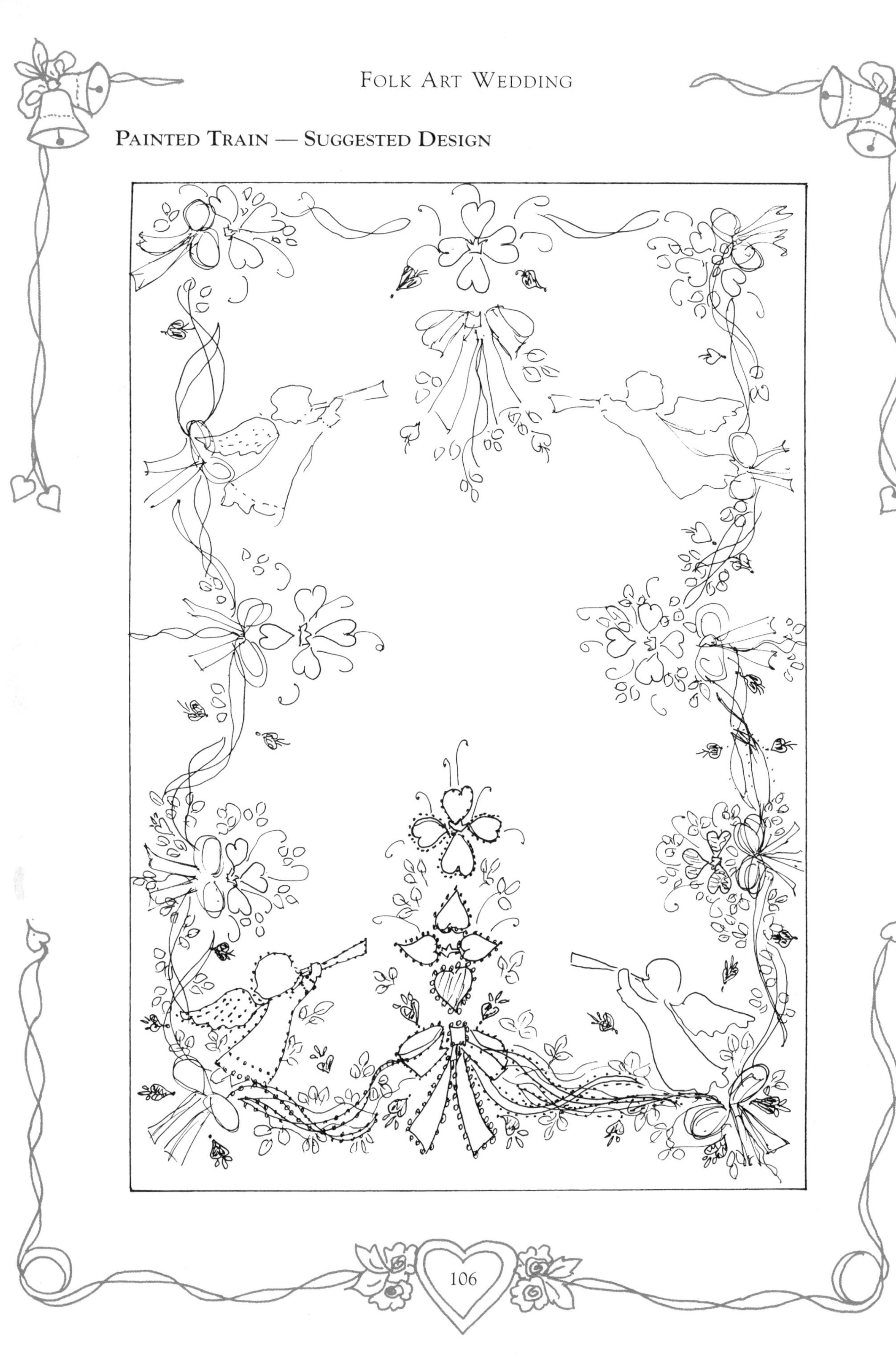

PAINTED TRAIN — STENCILS

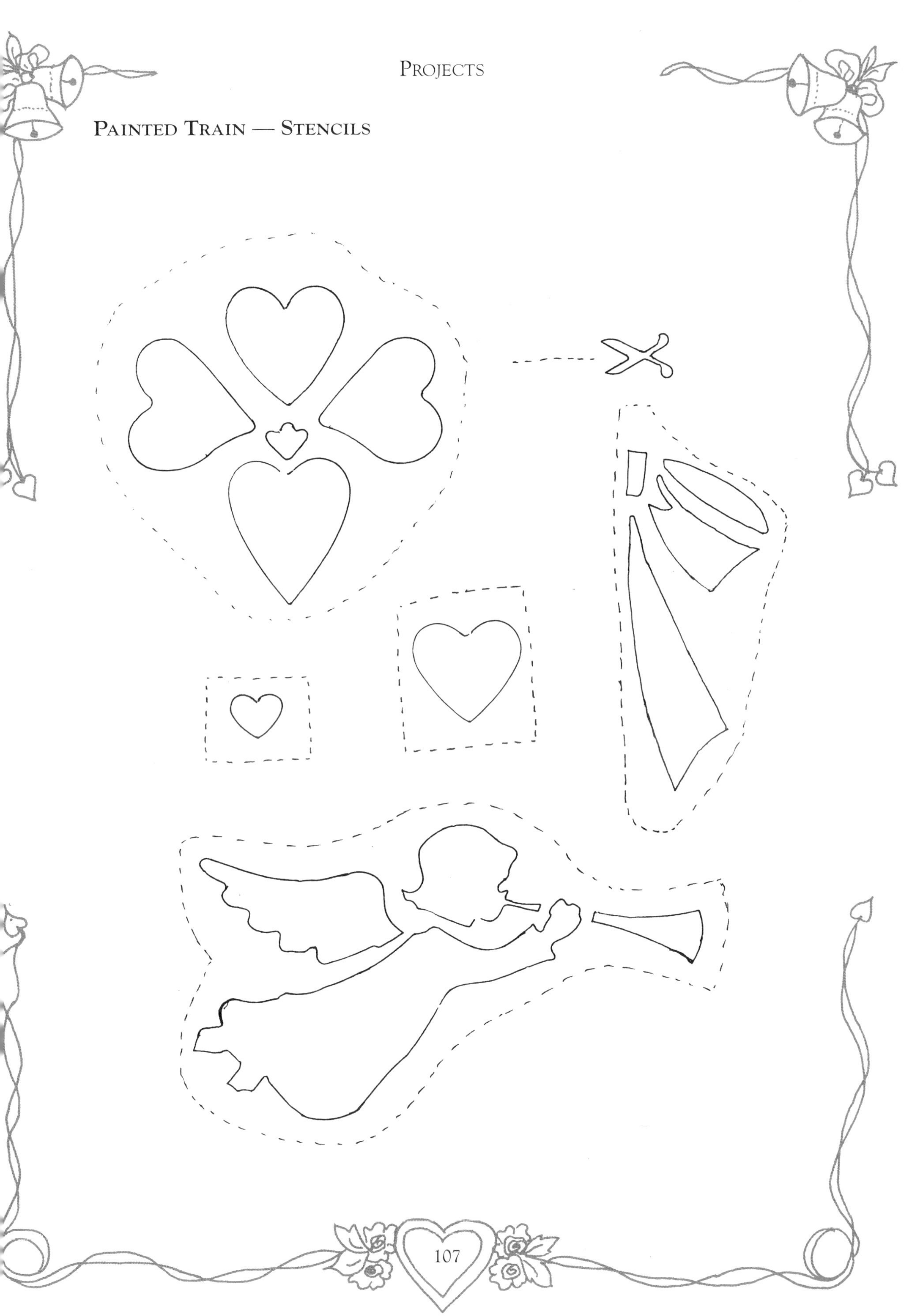

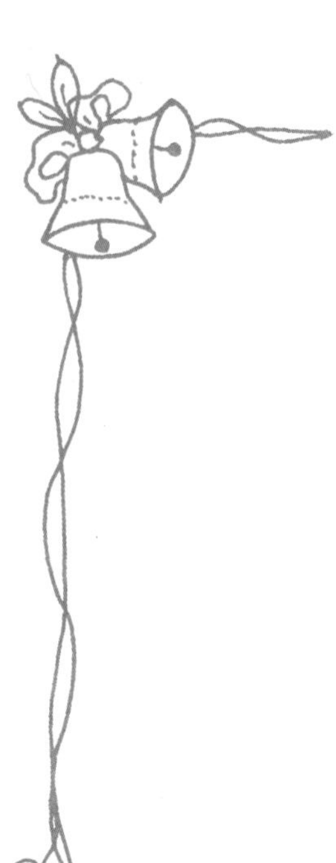

The Resort Case

Finding suitable cases to paint is not hard, and half the fun lies in the hunt. I have bought cases in secondhand shops, antique shops and church boutiques such as St Vinnies. On one occasion I found a beauty during the council clean-up. You may prefer to paint on a new case.

I love painting cases. I have painted old hat cases, old bowls cases and leather cases — all surfaces will take painting. The final surface is varnished, protecting your beautiful painting. Travelling, particularly flying, is not a problem. Airport staff normally tie a fragile label on the suitcase and put it in a special crate. And your luggage is never hard to find!

This is an exciting project. The case can be used to store your wedding dress or as a picnic basket. I am sure you will have lots of ideas. Please choose your favourite colours or use other combinations shown in this book.

TECHNIQUES

Sponging, faux fabric background, LAFS, dagger leaves, double-loaded strokes, dots, filler flowers and daisies

COLOURS

Rich Gold, Saphhire, Warm White, Storm Blue, French Blue, Teal Green, Green Oxide, Plum Pink, Burgundy

BRUSHES

Basecoater, fine liner, ⅛" dagger, Nos 3 and 5 round, rake or comb brush, ½"

OTHER MATERIALS

Wet and dry sandpaper, sealer (Jo Sonja's All Purpose Sealer), very fine steel wool, vinegar, sea or ceramic sponge, Kleister medium, nail brush, paper towels, water-based gloss varnish.

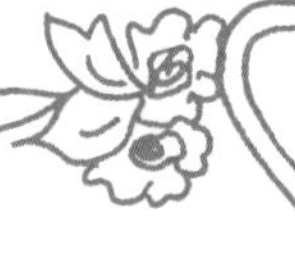
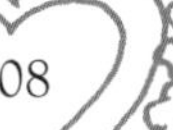

PREPARATION

1. If your case is old, air well, vacuum and wipe clean. Repair any damage. Naturally, you should closely inspect all hinges and locks. The keys are often long gone, but some repairers can renew fasteners. The lining can be removed and a new one put in. Or you could remove the lining altogether and paste in interesting papers. I have used old pianola rolls, old sheet music and wallpaper.

2. Sand and seal the case (at least two coats of sealer are needed).

3. Remove any rust from the metal hinges and locks with the steel wool. Clean, then paint with a 50:50 mix of water and vinegar. Dry well before sealing with an all-purpose sealer. When sealed, paint the locks and hinges with Rich Gold.

METHOD

1. Basecoat the sides of the case with Sapphire, and the base and lid with Warm White, at least two coats. The white will show through here and there to make the tapestry effect realistic.

2. Sponge around the side of the case, but not the lid, with Sapphire, Storm Blue, French Blue and Rich Gold. If you don't want to paint a design on the bottom of the case, sponge the bottom of the case too. Sponge a small area at a time until you like the effect. If necessary, retouch the locks and hinges with Rich Gold.

3. When doing the next step, do the base first, which can be a practice area. Have the nail brush and paper towels ready. Mix each of the blues with some Kleister medium, equal parts, in separate lids. Working quickly, sponge the darkest blue first, here and there, then the next darkest, working up to the lighter blues, using plenty of the mixture.

4. Wipe the nail brush straight across the entire base or lid. Make several stripes the width of the

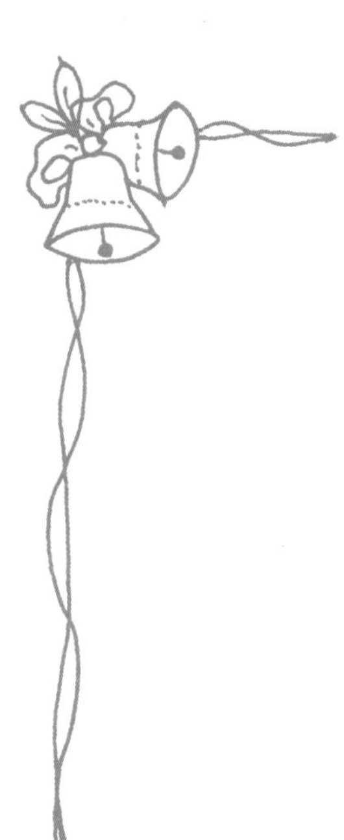

nail brush in the opposite direction, starting from the centre. Wipe off the excess paint from the brush and wipe three stripes, each the width of the brush, in the opposite direction, making squares. Allow to dry. The result should resemble woven checked fabric. I tend to rely on my eye, but please measure accurately and mark with a carbothello pencil where the stripes will go.

5. The rake brush needs a light touch and a little paint. Wipe off excess on paper towel. Practise first. Using the rake brush, alternate a Rich Gold stripe with a Sapphire stripe across, then a Gold Stripe with a French Blue stripe down the nail brush stripe. The rake brush will make finer stripes. The surface now resembles blue and gold striped fabric. Please refer to the design and the colour plate.

6. When the finish is dry, paint some LAFS trails, up and over and down and over the stripes in the different greens and Storm Blue. Paint

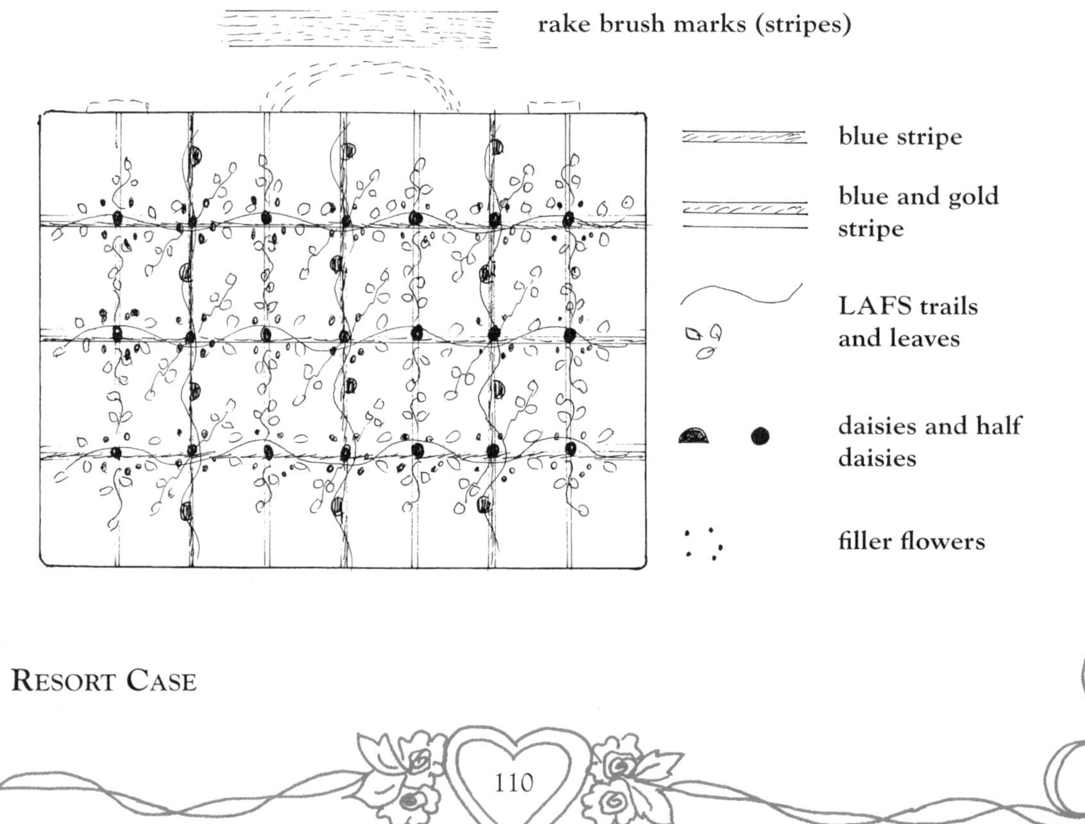

RESORT CASE

groups of three small dagger leaves, then single leaves along these trails in different greens and Storm Blue. Paint veins in different colours.

Note: This stage and the following flower painting should be done in a regular pattern, if you wish to have a woven floral tapestry effect. This is how the material would be woven. The coloured warp and weft threads are placed on the loom and woven in a particular sequence.

7. With the No.3 round brush, paint the daisies, half daisies and buds with small double-loaded strokes of Plum Pink and Warm White. The centres are Burgundy and Warm White dots. (Refer to the colour plate.)

8. The small forget-me-nots or filler flowers are done with the tip of the No.3 round brush, using Sapphire and Warm White. Just tip the brush into the two colours and push five little petals. The centres are dots of Rich Gold.

9. Paint a tie-on wooden label if needed. Basecoat, and add filler flowers and your initials.

10. Varnishing will protect all your beautiful painting and make the surface stronger.

I do hope you found this a fascinating painting experience. I am quite sure that wherever you go, your case will be greatly admired. Well done, and have a wonderful trip.

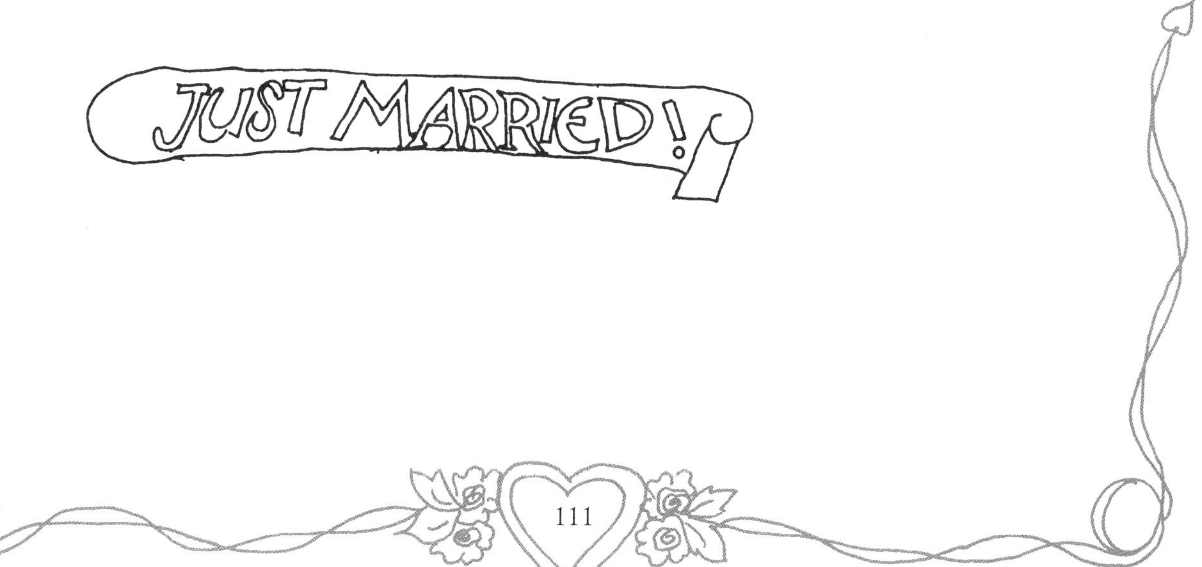

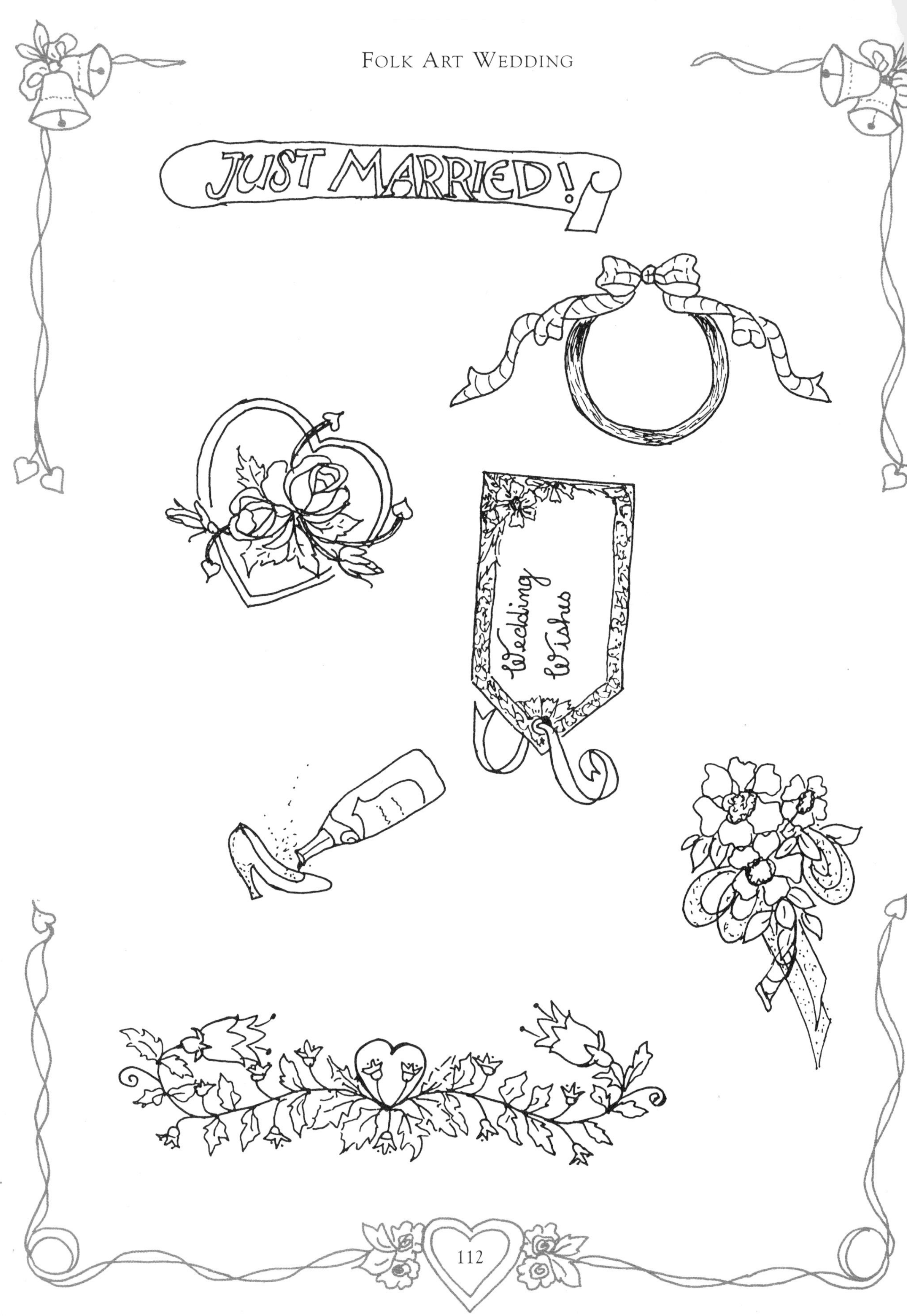
JUST MARRIED!
Wedding Wishes